CONTENTS

Page 4 EGGS and CHEESE
How to separate eggs
Page 5 Scrambled eggs
Page 6 Omelette
Page 7 Spanish omelette
Page 8 Orange omelette
Page 9 French toast
Page 10 Pancakes
Page 12 Croque monsieur (French ham and cheese sandwich)
Page 13 Cheese ramekin
Page 14 Cheese potato cakes
Page 15 Cheese straws
Page 16 Cheese soufflé

Page 18 MEAT and FISH
Page 19 Baked fish
Page 20 Oven-fried chicken
Page 21 Salmon Kedgeree (Anglo-Indian fish and rice dish)
Page 22 Creamed chicken on toast
Page 23 Risotto (Italian rice dish)
Page 24 Toad-in-the-Hole (English sausages in batter)
Page 25 Jewish beef pot roast
Page 26 Moussaka (Greek meat, potato and tomato casserole)
Page 28 Meat balls in cabbage leaves
Page 30 Goulash (Hungarian meat stew)
Page 32 Pork in sweet and sour sauce
Page 33 Spaghetti and meat balls

Page 34 VEGETABLES
White sauce
Page 35 Rice
Page 36 Salads and French dressing
Page 37 Waldorf Salad
Page 38 Vichy carrots (French candied carrots)
Page 39 Mashed potatoes
Page 40 Baked potatoes
Page 41 Potatoes and onions
Page 42 Potato cakes
Page 43 Colcannon (Irish mashed potatoes and cabbage)

Page 44 PUDDINGS and DESSERTS
Fried bananas
Page 45 Orange mousse
Page 46 Lemon fondant sweets (candies)
Page 47 American apple pie
Page 48 Fruit Kuchen (German fruit tart)

Page 50 BAKING
Scotch krispies
Page 51 Melting lemon or chocolate drops.
Page 52 Semolina shortbread cookies
Page 54 Raisin scones
Page 55 Chocolate kisses
Page 56 Chocolate surprise cake
Page 57 Chocolate butter icing (frosting)
Page 58 Lazy daisy cake
Page 59 Brown soda bread
Page 60 Pastry–traditional method
Page 61 Pastry–new fast method
Page 62 Lemon meringue pie
Page 64 Jam Tarts

EGGS AND CHEESE

Apart from being delicious, both eggs and cheese are very, very versatile to cook with. The main thing to remember is not to overcook either of them.

How to separate eggs

You will need:

an egg of course!

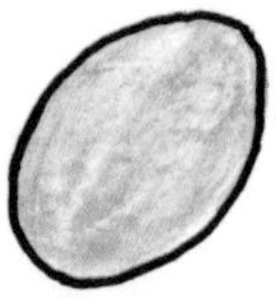

a bowl and a cup

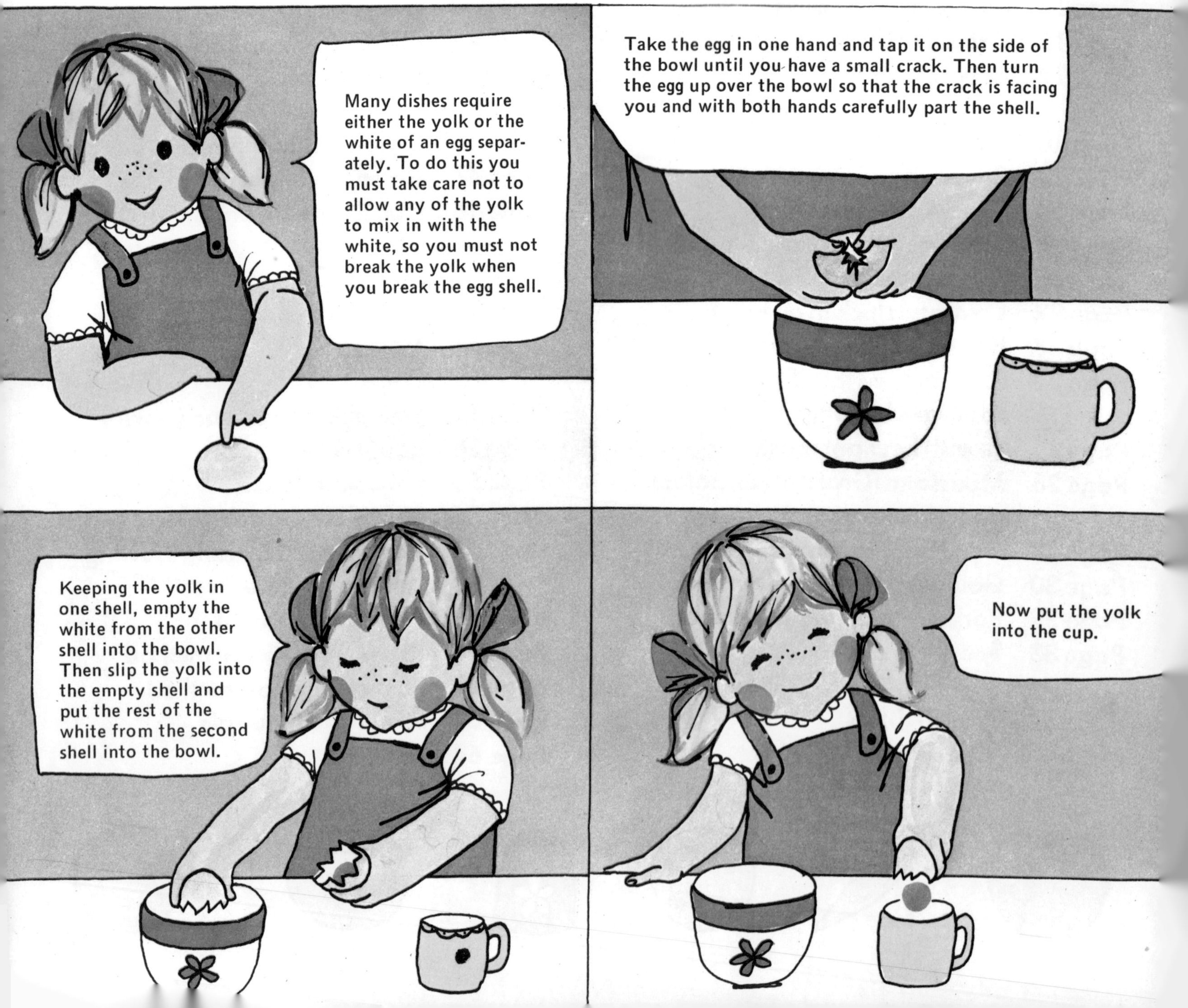
Many dishes require either the yolk or the white of an egg separately. To do this you must take care not to allow any of the yolk to mix in with the white, so you must not break the yolk when you break the egg shell.
Take the egg in one hand and tap it on the side of the bowl until you have a small crack. Then turn the egg up over the bowl so that the crack is facing you and with both hands carefully part the shell.
Keeping the yolk in one shell, empty the white from the other shell into the bowl. Then slip the yolk into the empty shell and put the rest of the white from the second shell into the bowl.
Now put the yolk into the cup.

Scrambled Eggs

Delicious for breakfast or supper.

For each person you will need:

2 eggs

a pinch of salt and a shake of pepper

½ an eggshell full of milk

½ ounce (1 tablespoon) of butter

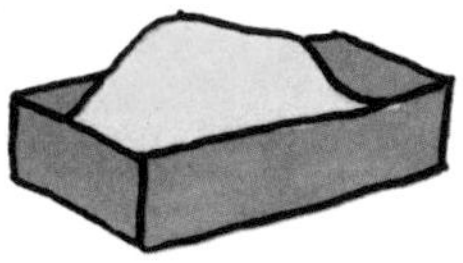

a slice of buttered toast

1 bowl

1 egg whisk

1 thick-bottomed pan

1 wooden spoon

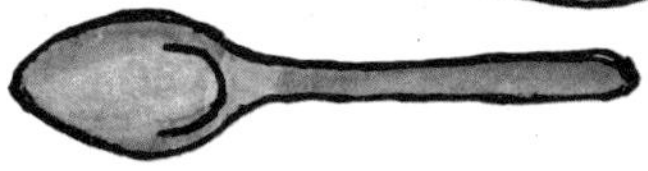

Break the eggs into the bowl and whisk lightly with the salt, pepper and milk.
Melt the butter in the pan and pour in the eggs. Stir very gently with the wooden spoon and keep the heat low.
Keep turning the eggs, taking care to loosen them as soon as they start to set at the bottom of the pan. They should be light and creamy. Take care not to overcook.
Serve at once with hot buttered toast.

Omelette

This is very quick to make and you may add a variety of goodies to an omelette. Make a plain one first and then experiment when you can do this well.

For each person you will need:

- 2 eggs
- a pinch of salt and a shake of pepper
- ½ an eggshell of water
- ½ ounce (1 tablespoon) of butter

- 1 bowl
- 1 egg whisk
- 1 fork
- 1 omelette pan or small frying pan
- 1 fish slice (spatula)

Break the eggs into the bowl and add salt, pepper and water. Whisk gently.
Heat the butter in the pan and pour in the eggs. Turn down the heat a little.
As the eggs begin to set at the bottom of the pan, lift the sides with the fork and let the runny egg run under.
When it's all just set, fold it over and serve immediately, on a warm plate. It is lovely eaten with a salad (page 36) and home-baked brown soda bread (page 59).

Spanish Omelette

Here is one of the many different omelettes you may make.

For each person you will need:

½ an onion

2 small or 1 large tomato

some hot water

a small piece of green pepper
or a few peas

1 ounce (2 tablespoons) of butter

2 eggs

a pinch of salt and a shake of pepper

½ an eggshell of water

1 sharp knife

1 chopping board

1 omelette pan or
small frying pan

1 plate

1 egg whisk   1 bowl

1 fork

1 fish slice (spatula)

Peel and chop the onion. Leave the tomato in very hot water for a few minutes (this makes it easier to peel). Peel and chop the tomato. And the piece of green pepper.
Mind your fingers.
Fry the vegetables very gently in half the butter until they are soft and cooked through. Put them on a plate and keep warm in a low oven.
Make the omelette as shown on page 6.
When the omelette is cooked, put the vegetables in the centre and fold it over like this. It's good served with salad and brown bread.

Orange Omelette

This is an omelette that Portuguese children look forward to for their pudding.

For one omelette (you cut it in half for 2 people) you will need:

2 eggs

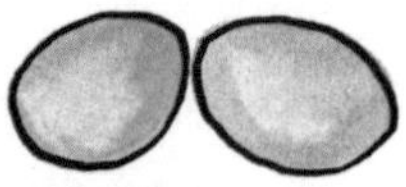

2 ounces ($\frac{1}{4}$ cup) of sugar

$\frac{1}{2}$ an orange

$\frac{1}{2}$ ounce (1 tablespoon) of butter

a little castor sugar (superfine)

1 bowl

1 fruit squeezer

1 egg whisk

1 omelette pan or small frying pan

1 fish slice (spatula)

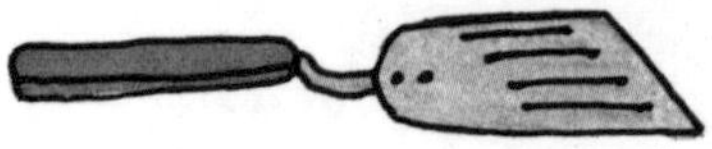

Break the eggs into the bowl and add the sugar.
Squeeze the orange and pour the juice into the bowl. Whisk up.
Heat the butter in the pan and when it begins to bubble, pour in the egg mixture. Turn down the heat.
As the egg begins to set, lift the sides and let the runny egg go underneath. Repeat this all around until all the runny egg has gone, and the omelette is just cooked but not too dry. Sprinkle with a little castor sugar (superfine) and serve immediately.
You can share it with your friends.

French Toast

Canadian children enjoy this for breakfast or supper with grilled (broiled) bacon rashers (slices) and maple syrup or honey.

For each person you will need:

1 egg

a pinch of salt and a shake of pepper

1 thick slice of white bread (remove crusts)

1 ounce (2 tablespoons) of margarine

2 bacon rashers (slices)

maple syrup or honey

1 egg whisk

1 bowl

2 plates

1 frying pan

1 fish slice (spatula)

1 knife

Place the bread on a plate. Whisk the egg lightly with the salt and pepper and pour it over the bread. Leave for 15 minutes and then turn it over to soak until all the egg is used up.
Melt the margarine in the pan and fry the bread on both sides until it is golden brown. You could grill (broil) the bacon while the bread is frying.
Place the bread on a warm plate and spread it with maple syrup or honey.
Yum.
Place the bacon on top and serve at once. Canadian children have great ideas!

Pancakes

Pancakes are made from a basic batter mixture which will also make Yorkshire pudding, Toad-in-the-hole, and other goodies.

For 5 pancakes you will need:

4 ounces (1 cup) of plain flour

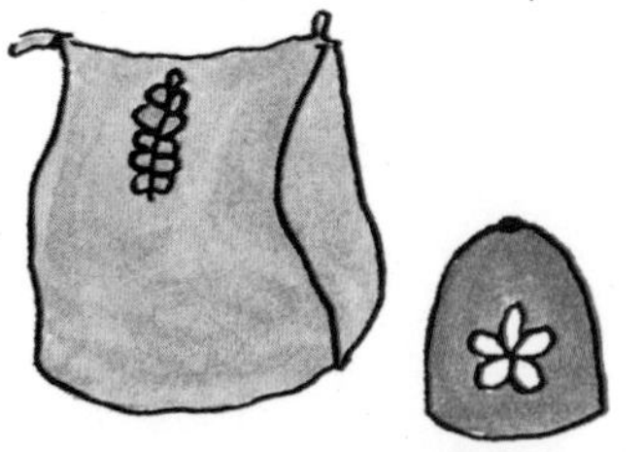

1/4 teaspoon of salt

1 egg

1/2 pint (1 1/4 cups) of milk

2 ounces (1/4 cup) of margarine

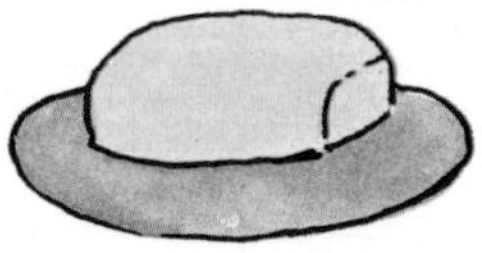

For the filling:

Maple syrup, or honey, or jam,

or castor sugar (superfine)

and lemon juice

Sift the flour and salt into the bowl.

Make a hole in the centre of the flour and break the egg into it. Mix well with the fork.

Gradually add the milk, stirring well. Beat the mixture with the egg whisk for 5 minutes. Hard work!
Your friend could help.

Heat 1 teaspoon of margarine in the pan. When it begins to smoke slightly, turn down the heat.

1 sieve

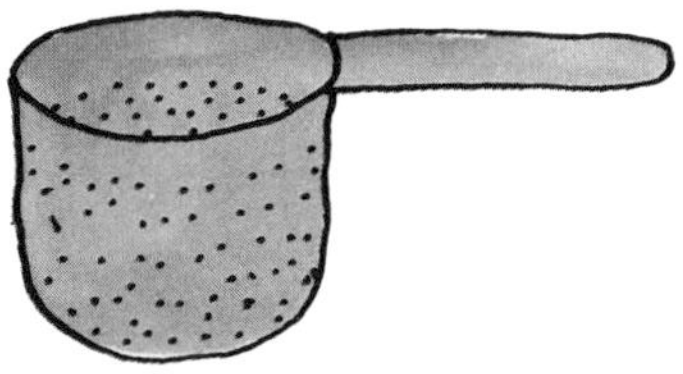

1 tablespoon

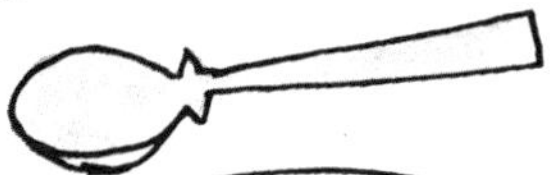

1 bowl

1 fork

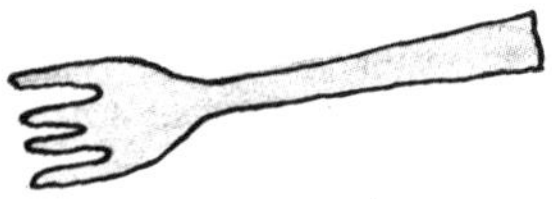

1 egg whisk

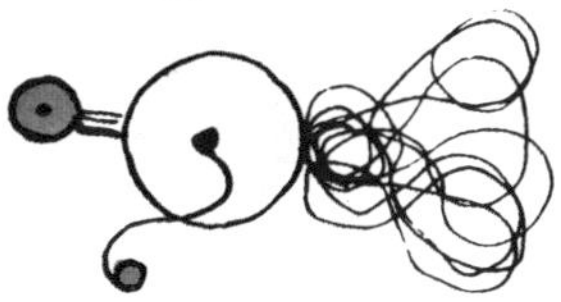

1 teaspoon

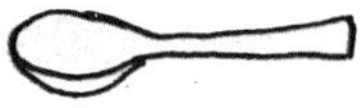

1 10 inch frying pan

1 fish slice (spatula)

a warm plate

Pour 5 tablespoons of the mixture into the centre of the pan.

Gently tip the pan in a circle until the mixture completely covers the bottom.

When the top is just dry, turn it over and cook the other side. Lift the edge of the pancake to see when it is nicely brown underneath. Put it on a plate in a warm oven.

Repeat pictures 4, 5, 6, and 7 with the rest of the mixture. Fold like this, with the honey, syrup, jam, or juice and sugar in the middle.

Croque Monsieur

In France, young French children love to eat this.

For each person you will need:

2 slices of white bread, buttered

1 slice of cooked ham, same size as the bread

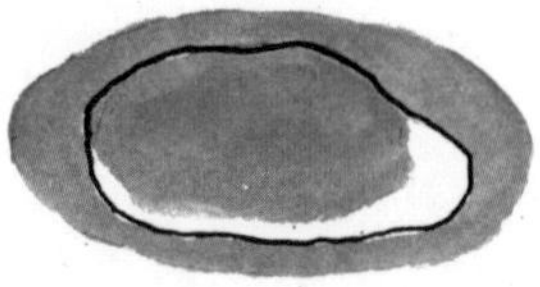

1 slice of cheese, same size as the bread

1 ounce (2 tablespoons) of margarine

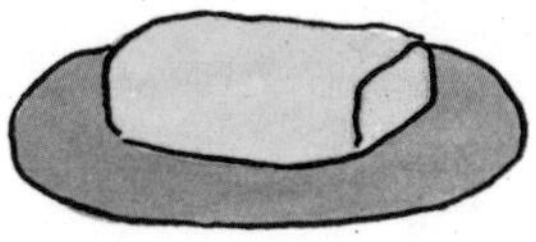

1 frying pan

1 knife

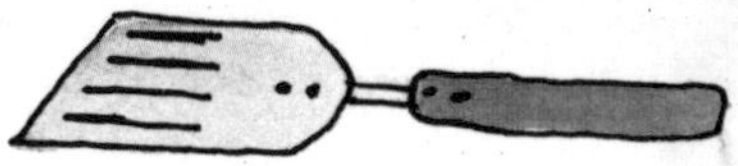

1 fish slice (spatula)

Trim the crust off the bread. Make a sandwich with the buttered side of the bread on the outside and the slices of ham and cheese inside.
Heat the margarine in the pan. When it is melted, turn the heat down to low.
Fry the sandwich until it is lovely and brown on both sides. The cheese will go soft inside.
Serve immediately.
Mind you don't burn your tongue!

Cheese Ramekin

In Switzerland this is a favourite with most children when they come in from the cold and snow.

For 4 people you will need:

4 slices of white bread, buttered

a little margarine

4 ounces (1 cup) of cheese

½ pint (1¼ cups) of milk

¼ teaspoon of grated or ground nutmeg

a pinch of salt and a shake of pepper

1 egg

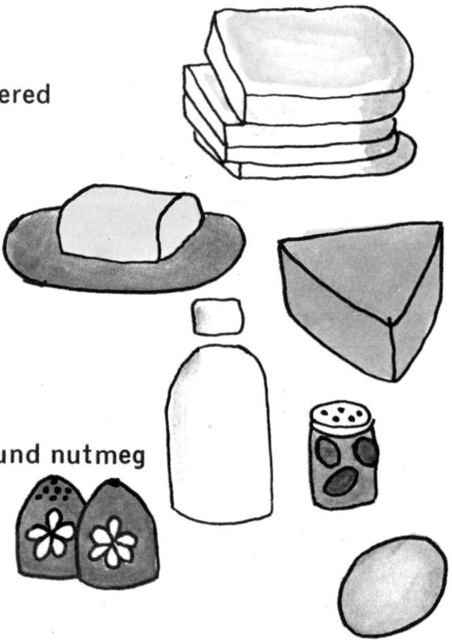

1 knife

1 ramekin or 1½ pint casserole dish

1 cheese grater

1 saucepan

1 egg whisk

ON OVEN
et the
ven at
50°F,
as Mark
Cut
ch slice
bread
to 4
Cut the cheese into 4 pieces and grate each piece. Grease the dish with the margarine.
Arrange the bread and cheese alternately in the dish, starting and finishing with the bread and leaving one lot of cheese.
Heat the milk, and before it
ubbles up and boils, remove
rom the heat and add the
utmeg, salt, pepper and egg.
Whisk. Pour the milk over the
read.
Sprinkle the remaining cheese on top. Place in the oven for 45 minutes, till the top is crisp and brown.
OVEN OFF

Cheese Potato Cakes

These are very good for little people who are growing into big ones.

For 8 cakes you will need:

½ pound of potatoes
(2 medium ones)

2 ounces (½ cup) of cheese

½ ounce (½ tablespoon) of butter

¼ teaspoon of salt and a shake of pepper

a shake of cayenne pepper

2 ounces (½ cup) of plain flour

a little flour for rolling out

1 ounce (2 tablespoons) of margarine

1 potato peeler

1 knife

1 saucepan

1 sieve or colander

1 cheese grater

1 potato masher or large fork

1 rolling pin

1 frying pan

1 palette knife (spatula)

Peel the potatoes and cut them in half. Put them in a saucepan and cover them with water. Put the lid on. Boil till soft and then drain into the sieve.
Grate the cheese. Mash together the potatoes, butter, cheese, salt, pepper and flour. Leave to cool for a few minutes.
Gather the mixture together with your hands. Sprinkle a little flour on the table and roll out the mixture with a rolling pin until it is ½ an inch thick.
Cut it into 8 squares and fry these in the margarine until both sides are crispy golden.
Anyone around will help you eat them.

Cheese Straws

These are great for a party. If your parents are having a party, ask them if they would like you to make these cheese straws. Add a little extra cayenne pepper if they accept the invitation.

For about 24 straws you will need:

6 ounces (1½ cups) of plain flour

4 tablespoons (5 tablespoons) of vegetable oil

2 tablespoons (2½ tablespoons) of water

2 ounces (½ cup) of grated cheese

¼ teaspoon of salt

a few shakes of cayenne pepper

a little flour for rolling out

margarine for greasing the baking tray

1 tablespoon

1 teaspoon

a cheese grater

1 bowl

1 wooden spoon

1 rolling pin

1 large baking tray

1 knife

ON OVEN
Set the oven at 425°F, Gas Mark 7. Place the flour, oil, water, grated cheese, salt and pepper in a bowl and stir well. The mixture will be stiff so it will be hard work. You may use your hands to get it into a round ball.
Knead it together as if you were working plasticine or playdough. When it is smooth, shake the flour onto the table and rolling pin, and roll the dough until it is ¼ of an inch thick. Grease the baking tray with margarine.
Cut the pastry into strips about 4 inches wide. Then cut the 4 inch strips into ¼ inch fingers.
Lay the fingers on the baking tray ¼ of an inch apart and cook for 15 minutes. Write down the time you put them in the oven. Remove from the tray when they are cold.
Good eating!
OVEN OFF

Cheese Soufflé

For lunch or supper. Many adults think this French dish is difficult to make — but it isn't if you know how!

For 2 or 3 people you will need:

margarine to grease the dish

3 eggs

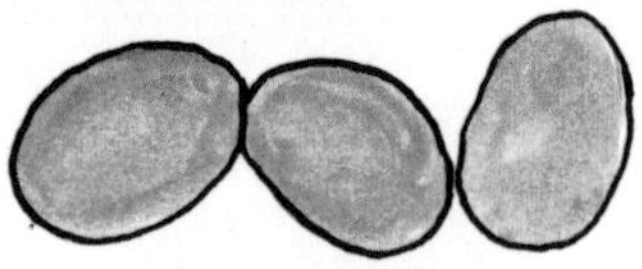

1 ounce (2 tablespoons) of butter

1 level tablespoon (1¼ tablespoons) of flour

¼ pint (½ cup + 2 tablespoons) of milk

a pinch of salt and a shake of pepper

3 ounces (¾ cup) of cheese

a soufflé or deep casserole dish about 6 inches across

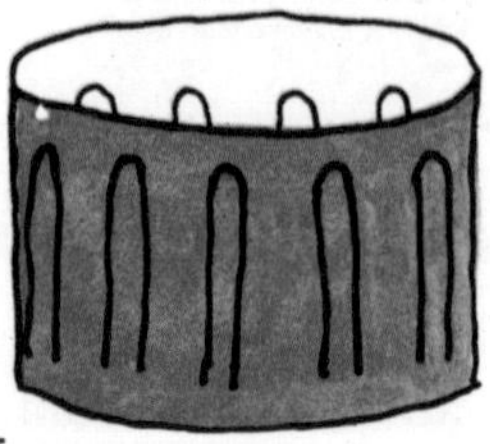

a 3 X 24 inch strip of greaseproof paper (wax-paper or foil)

ON
OVEN
Set the oven at 400°F, Gas Mark 6. Grease the dish and tie the paper (foil) around it, like this.

Separate the egg yolks from the whites as instructed on page 4. Place the white in the bowl and the yolks in the cup.

Melt the butter in the pan over a low heat. Stir in the flour. Remove from heat. Add the milk, a little at a time, and stir with the wooden spoon. Add salt and pepper.

Bring the mixture to the boil, stirring constantly. When it thickens, turn off the heat. Beat in the egg yolks with the wooden spoon.
(If it goes lumpy you'll have to whisk it!)

string

scissors

adhesive tape

1 large bowl

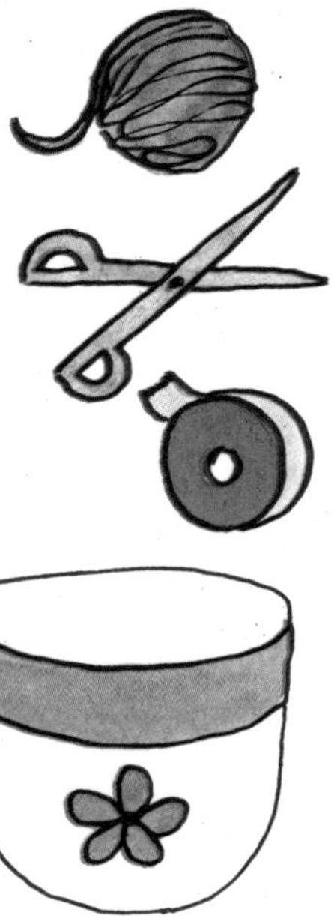

1 cup

1 small saucepan

1 wooden spoon

1 cheese grater

1 egg whisk

Grate the cheese and add to the mixture. Stir.
Beat the egg whites until you can turn the bowl upside down without them falling out.
Carefully though, they might not be stiff enough!
Pour the contents of the saucepan into the big bowl with the egg whites and blend gently with the wooden spoon. Pour into the dish.
Place it in the oven and write down the time you put it in. Don't open the oven while it is cooking or your soufflé will go flat! Bake for 30 minutes. Remove the paper before serving with vegetables or salad and rolls.

MEAT AND FISH

Most of the recipes in this section are cooked in a casserole dish. This is because it is safer, more interesting, more economical, very nourishing, and also you will be able to experiment more easily. As you become more familiar with these dishes, you will be able to invent your own recipes.

You will find that before you become used to cutting up onions you will cry every time you do so. Not because it hurts of course! To avoid being a tearful cook you can place the sliced onions in a bowl of cold water until you are ready to use them. This prevents the onion vapour from stinging your eyes and making them 'water'. Before chopping onions, cut off and discard both ends. And always wash your hands after chopping onions.

If you find that your guests are not ready when your casserole dish has finished cooking, don't panic! Simply turn the oven down very low (about 200°F, Gas Mark ¼) and it will keep hot without spoiling until they are ready to eat.

Baked Fish

Any filleted white fish would do for this recipe. Cod, sole or plaice (flounder) would be excellent.

For each person you will need:

a little margarine to grease the casserole dish

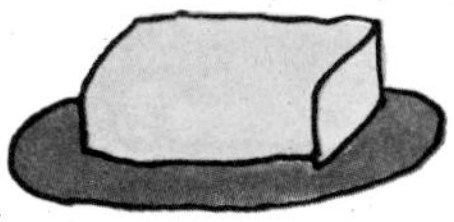

1 fish (about 8 ounces)

2 tomatoes

a pinch of salt and a shake of pepper

juice of ½ a lemon

1 ounce (2 tablespoons) of butter

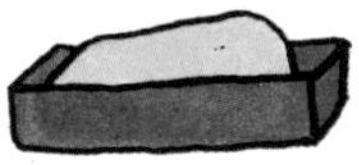

1 tablespoon (1¼ tablespoons) of single (light) cream

1 casserole with lid

1 knife

1 chopping board

1 fork

1 tablespoon

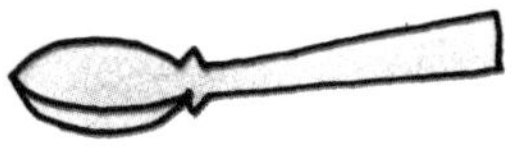

ON
OVEN
Set the oven at 375°F, Gas Mark 5. Grease the casserole dish. Place the fish in the casserole.

Slice the tomatoes and lay them neatly on the fish. Sprinkle with salt, pepper and lemon juice. Put little pieces of butter dotted over the tomatoes. Put the lid on the casserole.

Bake in the oven for about 20 minutes. Test with a fork to see if the fish is cooked. Leave it a little longer if it needs more cooking time.

Take off the lid. Pour the cream on the tomatoes and place under a hot grill (broiler) for 5 minutes.
Serve now.
OVEN

Oven-Fried Chicken

A favourite recipe that American children enjoy especially when they wrap it in foil and take it on a picnic.

For each person you will need:

1 ounce (2 tablespoons) of butter

1 tablespoon (1¼ tablespoons) of flour

a pinch of salt and a shake of pepper

½ teaspoon of paprika

1 joint (serving piece) of chicken

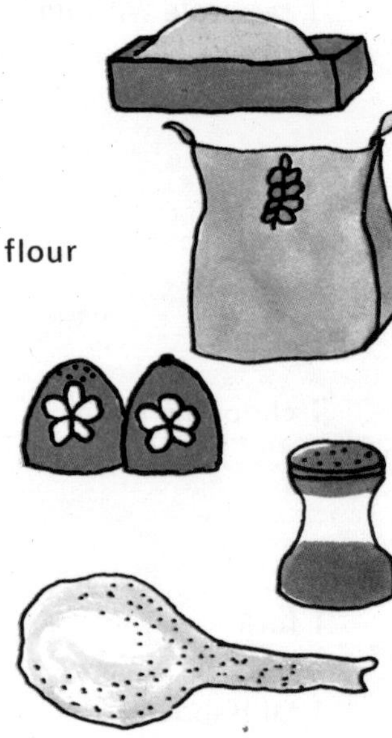

1 roasting pan

1 tablespoon

1 teaspoon

1 paper bag

1 fork

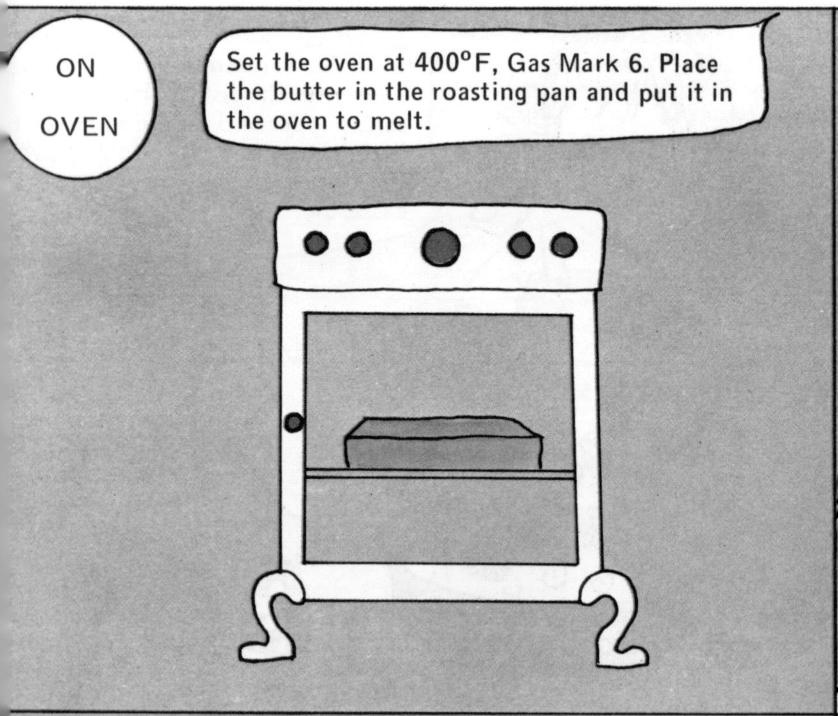
ON OVEN
Set the oven at 400°F, Gas Mark 6. Place the butter in the roasting pan and put it in the oven to melt.

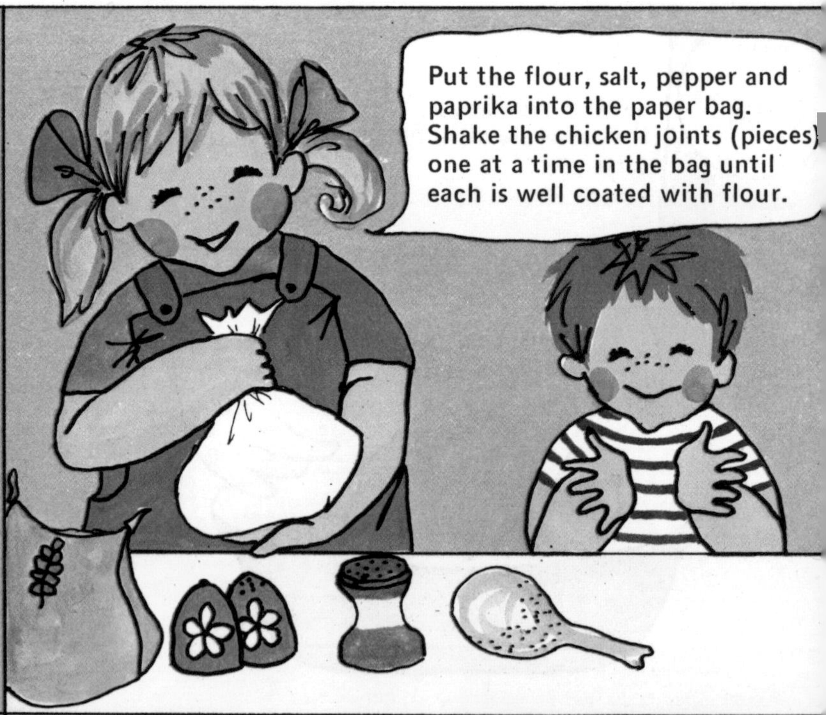
Put the flour, salt, pepper and paprika into the paper bag. Shake the chicken joints (pieces) one at a time in the bag until each is well coated with flour.

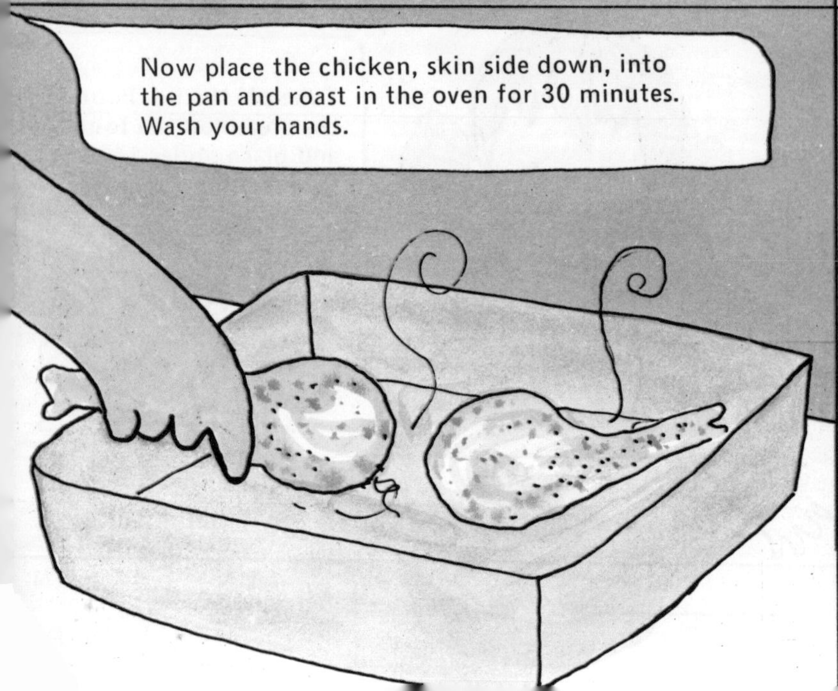
Now place the chicken, skin side down, into the pan and roast in the oven for 30 minutes. Wash your hands.

Turn the chicken pieces over and cook them for another 30 minutes.
Great eating!
OVEN OFF

Salmon Kedgeree

Kedgeree was originally an Anglo-Indian dish, but through the years it has been changed and adapted. There are several variations and this is one of them. You will need to know how the white sauce on page 34 is made and how to boil rice (page 35).

For 2 people you will need:

3 ounces (1/2 cup) of uncooked rice

the white sauce on page 34 (flour, salt, butter, milk)

1 egg

1 small tin (can) of salmon (about 8 ounces)

a pinch of salt and a shake of cayenne pepper

a pinch of mixed spices

a little parsley

2 lemon wedges

another shake of cayenne pepper

3 saucepans

1 tin (can) opener

1 knife

1 sieve

1 casserole dish

1 wooden spoon

3

ON
OVEN
Set the oven at 300°F, Gas Mark 2. Cook the rice as instructed on page 35 and leave it in the oven.
Follow the instructions for the roux sauce on page 34.
Boil the egg for 10 minutes and place it in cold water. Peel and slice it. Remove any bones and skin from the tinned (canned) salmon.
OVEN
OFF
Put all the ingredients except the lemon and parsley into the rice in the casserole dish and stir gently. Be careful not to break the salmon up too much. Leave in the oven for 10 minutes. Place a little chopped parsley on top of each portion and a lemon wedge on the side of each plate. Sprinkle with cayenne.

Creamed Chicken on Toast

22

A tasty snack that American children love to eat when they are quite hungry.

For 4 people you will need:

½ a cooked chicken

1 small onion

1 stick of celery

¼ of a green pepper

1½ ounces (3 tablespoons) of butter

4 slices of white bread

2 tablespoons (2½ tablespoons) of milk

1 tin (can) of condensed cream of chicken soup (about ½ pint (1¼ cups))

a sprig of parsley

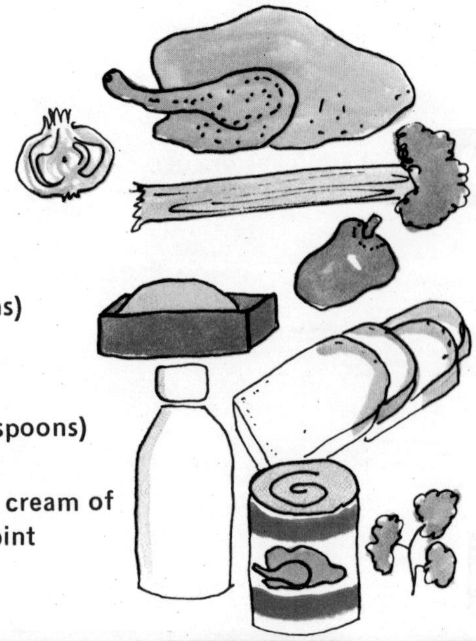

1 sharp knife

1 chopping board

1 frying pan

1 tablespoon

1 tin (can) opener

1 wooden spoon

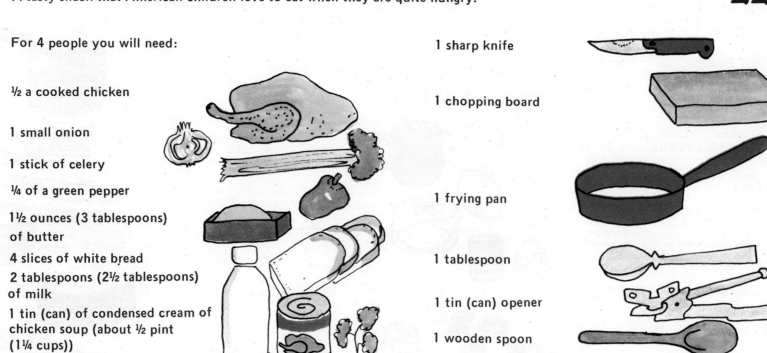

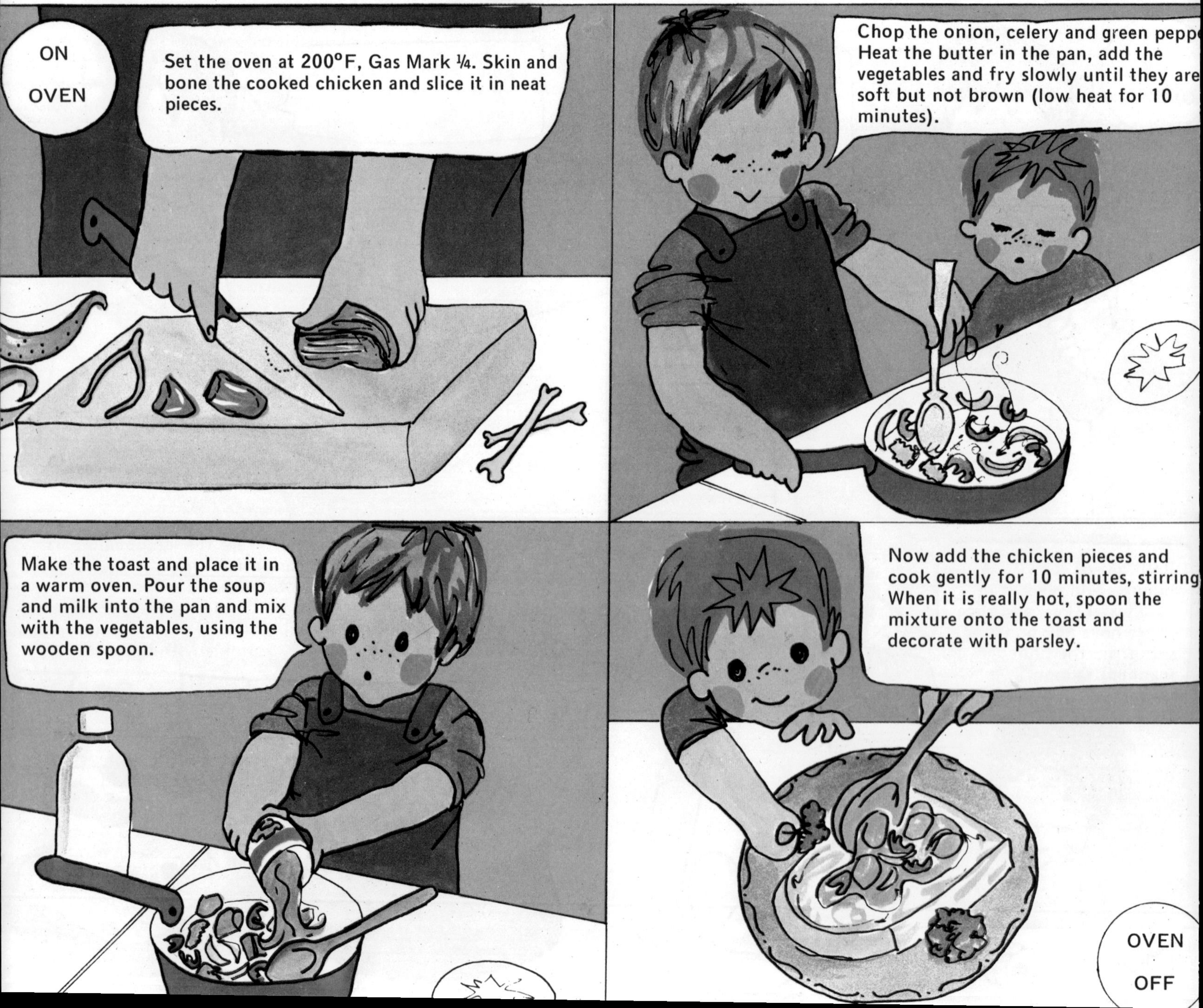
ON
OVEN
Set the oven at 200°F, Gas Mark ¼. Skin and bone the cooked chicken and slice it in neat pieces.
Chop the onion, celery and green pepp Heat the butter in the pan, add the vegetables and fry slowly until they are soft but not brown (low heat for 10 minutes).
Make the toast and place it in a warm oven. Pour the soup and milk into the pan and mix with the vegetables, using the wooden spoon.
Now add the chicken pieces and cook gently for 10 minutes, stirring. When it is really hot, spoon the mixture onto the toast and decorate with parsley.
OVEN
OFF

Risotto

All Italian children enjoy risotto for their lunch or supper.
This is quick to make and you can use your imagination to add all sorts of chopped cooked goodies if you like.

For 2 people you will need:

1 small onion (½ if large)
½ green pepper
6 small mushrooms
4 tomatoes
1½ ounces (3 tablespoons) of margarine
2 rashers (slices) of bacon
6 ounces (1 cup) of uncooked rice
1 pint (2½ cups) of stock, or water and a bouillon cube
2 ounces (2 tablespoons) of raw peas
a pinch of herbs

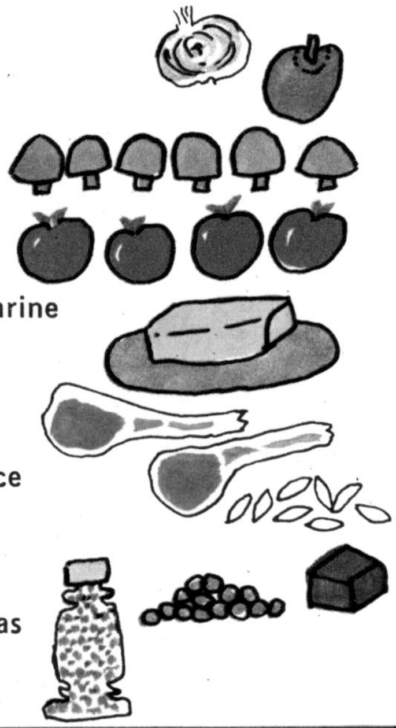

Extra ingredients, you may also add any of the following things:
chopped cooked chicken, ham, carrots, green beans, sweet corn or prawns (shrimps)

1 sharp knife
1 chopping board
1 frying pan with lid
1 fork

Slice the onion, pepper, mushrooms, tomatoes. Mind your fingers.
Fry the vegetables and bacon in the margarine till they are soft but not brown. Low heat. Add the rice and fry gently for 2 minutes. Pour in the stock, or bouillon cube dissolved in hot water.
Bring to the boil and add peas and herbs. Cover with lid and turn down the heat till it is just bubbling. You can hear it!
After 15 minutes taste the rice to see if it is cooked. Leave a little on a fork to cool before tasting. Add any extra ingredients now and heat for 1 minute after the rice is cooked.
Great served with a salad!

Toad-in-the-Hole

This makes a great lunch — and all children love it.

For 4 people you will need:

the batter on page 10 (flour, salt, egg and milk)

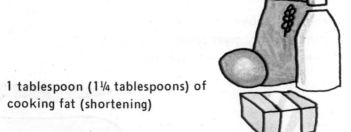

1 tablespoon (1¼ tablespoons) of cooking fat (shortening)

12 sausages, pork or beef

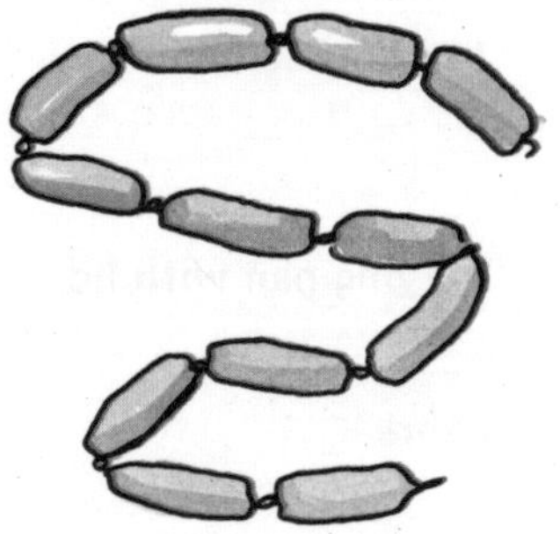

1 egg whisk

1 bowl

1 sieve

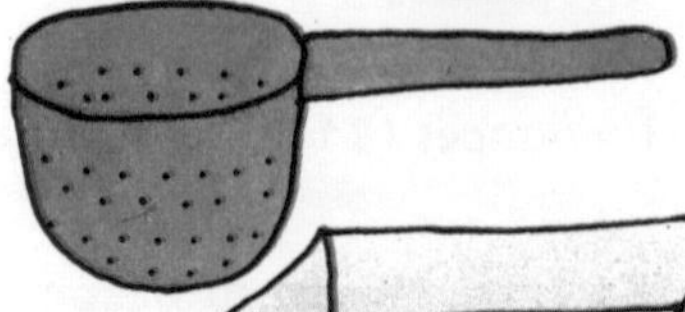

an 8 X 12 inch baking tin (pan) with deep sides

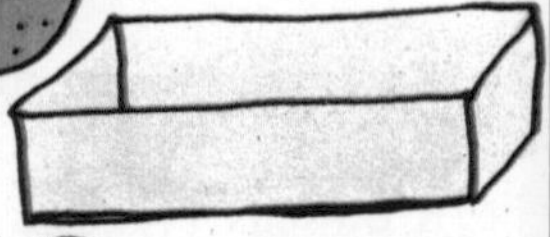

scissors

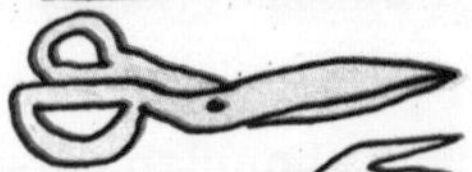

1 fork

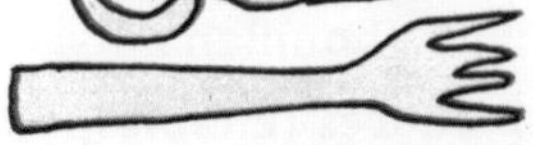

1 knife

ON
OVEN
Set the oven at 450°F, Gas Mark 8. Make the batter as shown on page 10 — you can add an extra egg if you like.

Put the cooking fat into the baking tin (pan) and place it in the oven. Separate the sausages. Prick each one twice and lay them evenly in the tin (pan) after the fat has melted. Bake for 10 minutes.

Pour the pancake mixture over the sausages. Cook for 35 minutes, at the top of the oven.
Don't peep!

When it is cooked, cut into four wedges and eat immediately. Good served with a green vegetable.
OVEN
OFF

Jewish Beef Pot Roast

This recipe is one way to make a large meal from an inexpensive but tasty cut of beef. It really is delicious and well worth the effort required to make it.

For a family of 6 you will need:

1 heaped tablespoon (1½ tablespoons) of flour

½ teaspoon of pepper

1 teaspoon of salt

3 pounds of chuck or rump beef

3 tablespoons (3¾ tablespoons) of vegetable oil

a stick of celery

1 large onion

1 pound of carrots

6 very small onions

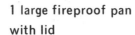

1 pint (2½ cups) of water

1 rounded tablespoon (1¼ tablespoons) of cornflour (cornstarch)

1 large fireproof pan with lid

1 knife

1 chopping board

1 large spare dish

1 teaspoon

1 tablespoon

Mix the flour, pepper and salt and roll the beef in this until it completely covers the meat. Heat the oil in the dish and brown the beef in it. Chop the celery and large onion into small pieces and brown them too.
Turn off the heat and allow the oil to cool down for 5 minutes. Now add ½ pint (1¼ cups) of water. Bring to the boil, turn down the heat so that the liquid is just bubbling, and put the lid on. Make a note of the time. Turn the beef occasionally during cooking time.Simmer for two hours.
eel and slice the carrots and eel the small onions. When the eef has been cooking for 2 ours, take it out of the pot and lace on a plate. Put the onions nd carrots in the pot. Now place he beef on top of them, and ut the lid back on. Cook for nother hour.
After an hour, place the beef and vegetables on a dish in a warm oven. Add another ½ pint (1¼ cups) of water to the juices in the pan. Mix cornflour (cornstarch) with a little water and add to the juices. Bring this to the boil stirring all the time. Place the gravy in a bowl with a spoon. Serve beef, vegetables and gravy with the potato cakes on page 42.

Moussaka

An everyday dish from Greece made with potatoes, minced (ground) meat and tomatoes.
Traditionally you would add aubergines (egg plants) but they can be very expensive and you might not like them.

For 2 people you will need:

1 sprig of parsley

1 onion

1½ ounces (3 tablespoons) of margarine

½ pound of minced (ground) lamb or beef

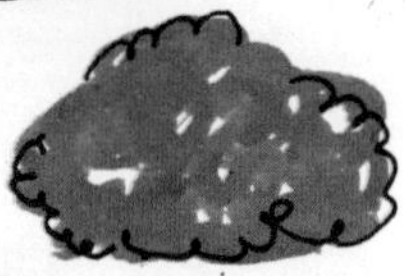

1 16 ounce tin (can) of tomatoes

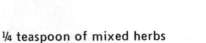

a pinch of salt and a shake of pepper

¼ teaspoon of mixed herbs

a little margarine for greasing

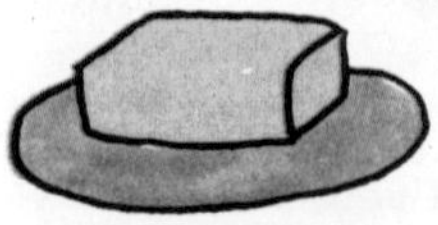

2 medium potatoes

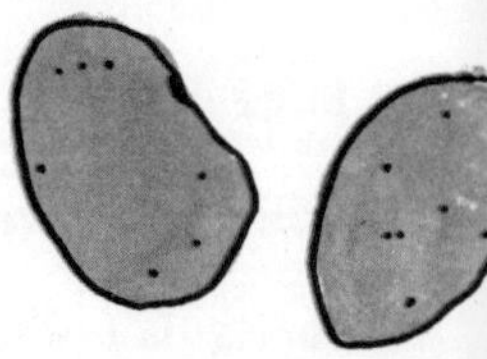

ON
OVEN
Set the oven at 350°F, Gas Mark 4. Chop the parsley and onion and fry them with the margarine and meat in the frying pan, separating the meat with the fork, until the meat changes colour.

Place the tomatoes from the tin (can) in a bowl. Add salt, pepper and herbs.

Grease the casserole dish. Peel the potatoes and slice them into thin rounds. Divide them into three portions.

Put a layer of potatoes in the bottom of the casserole and then place half of the meat mixture on top. Now add a layer of tomatoes.

For the sauce:

½ ounce (½ tablespoon) of butter

1 ounce (¼ cup) of flour

3 fluid ounces (¼ cup) of milk

½ raw egg, whisked

½ ounce (2 tablespoons) of grated cheese

1 knife

1 chopping board

1 frying pan

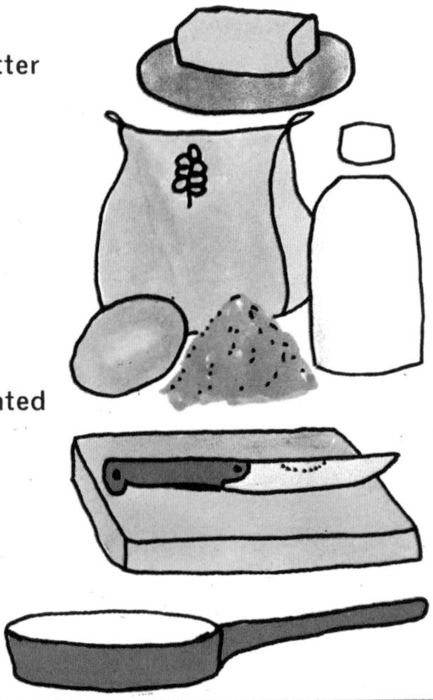

1 fork

1 tin (can) opener

1 bowl

1 teaspoon

1 saucepan

1 casserole with lid

1 egg whisk + bowl

1 cheese grater

1 wooden spoon

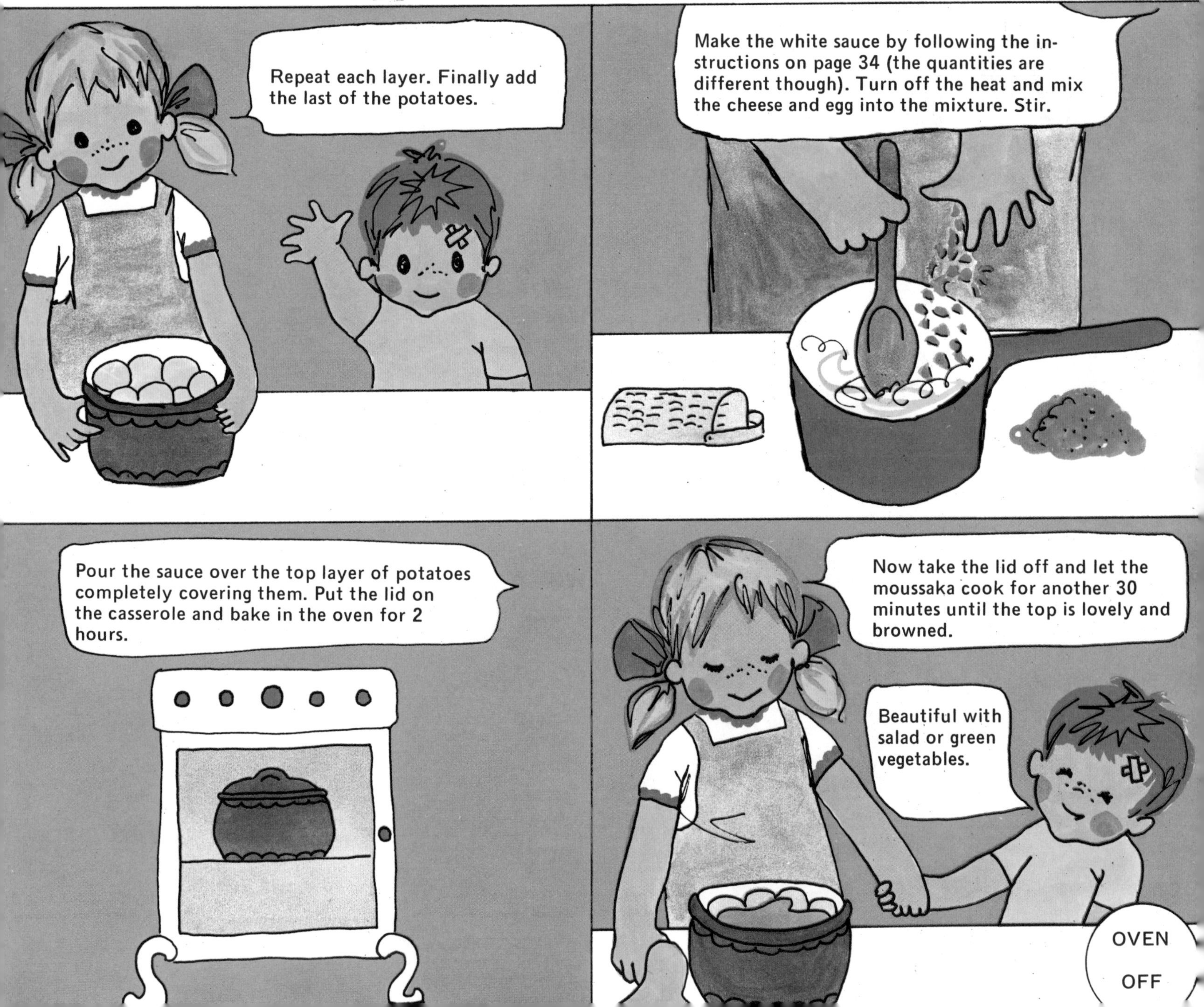
Repeat each layer. Finally add the last of the potatoes.
Make the white sauce by following the instructions on page 34 (the quantities are different though). Turn off the heat and mix the cheese and egg into the mixture. Stir.
Pour the sauce over the top layer of potatoes completely covering them. Put the lid on the casserole and bake in the oven for 2 hours.
Now take the lid off and let the moussaka cook for another 30 minutes until the top is lovely and browned.
Beautiful with salad or green vegetables.
OVEN OFF

Meat Balls in Cabbage Leaves

This dish comes from Turkey, where it is called Taraba. There, it is made with spinach leaves, which is better. But you may find it easier to use cabbage leaves.

For 2 hungry people you will need:

8 large cabbage or spinach leaves

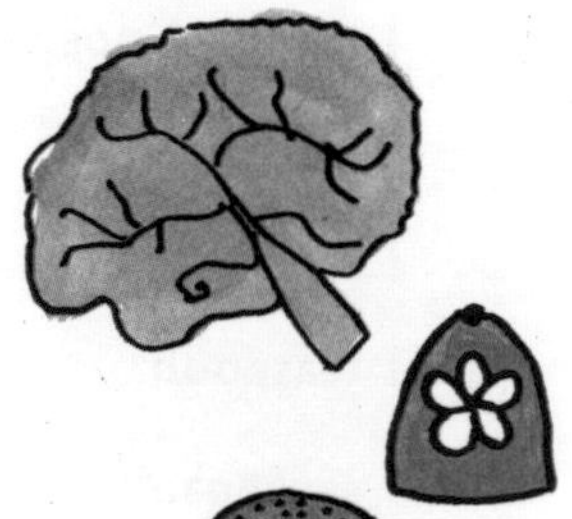

¼ level teaspoon of salt

¼ level teaspoon of paprika

¾ pound of minced (ground) lamb or beef

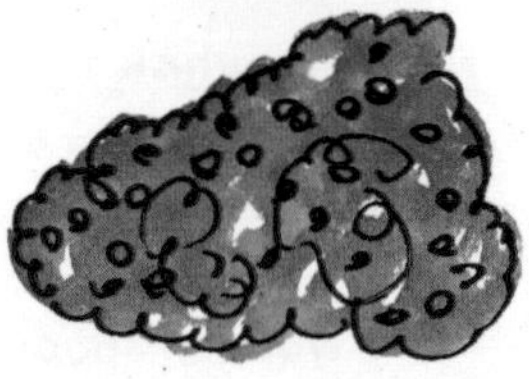

1½ ounces (3 tablespoons) of butter

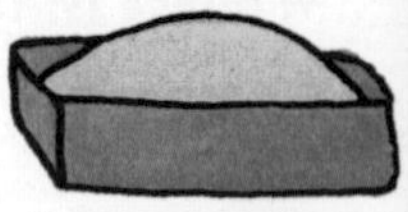

2½ tablespoons (3 tablespoons) of tomato ketchup

2½ tablespoons (3 tablespoons) of lemon juice

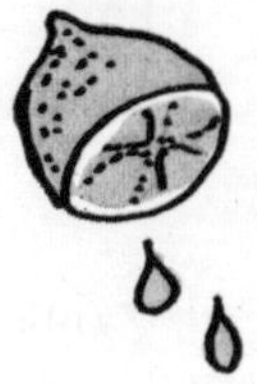

ON
OVEN
Set the oven at 375°F, Gas Mark 5. Wash the cabbage leaves and remove the stalks. Put the cabbage in the saucepan with a cupful of water. Bring to the boil. Cover with a lid and boil for 3 minutes.

Drain the cabbage and leave it to cool in the sieve.

Put the meat in the bowl and mix in the salt and paprika with a fork. Make the meat into 8 balls using your hands.

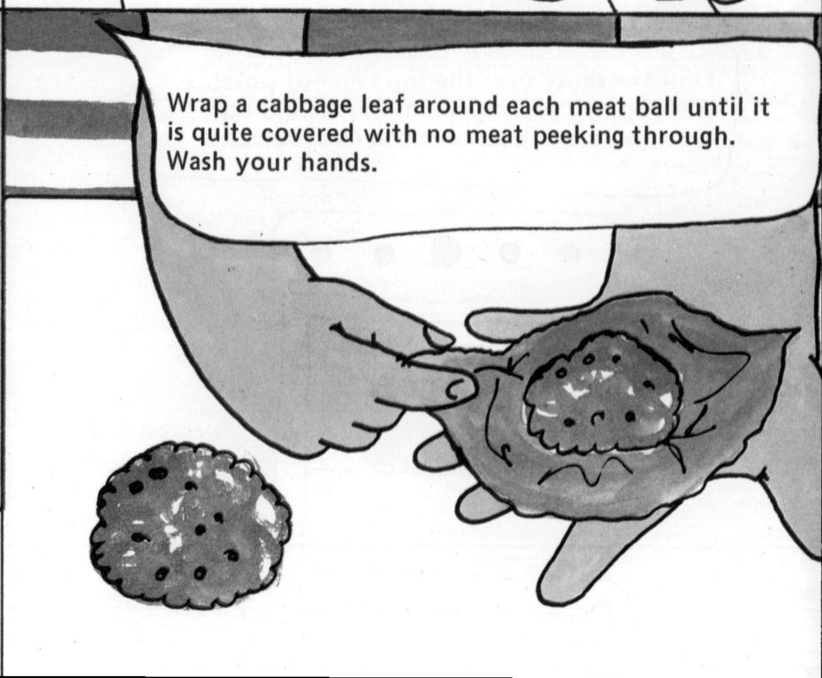
Wrap a cabbage leaf around each meat ball until it is quite covered with no meat peeking through. Wash your hands.

1 knife 

1 cup 

1 saucepan 

1 sieve 

1 bowl 

1 teaspoon 

1 fork 

1 tablespoon 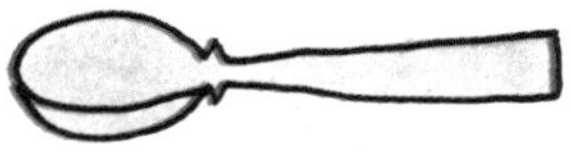

1 frying pan 

1 casserole dish with lid 

Melt the butter and ketchup in the frying pan. Add the stuffed cabbage leaves and brown them on both sides, turning with a tablespoon. Medium heat.

Put the cabbage parcels into the casserole. Add lemon juice to the juices in the frying pan and pour in all the liquid. Put the lid on the casserole.

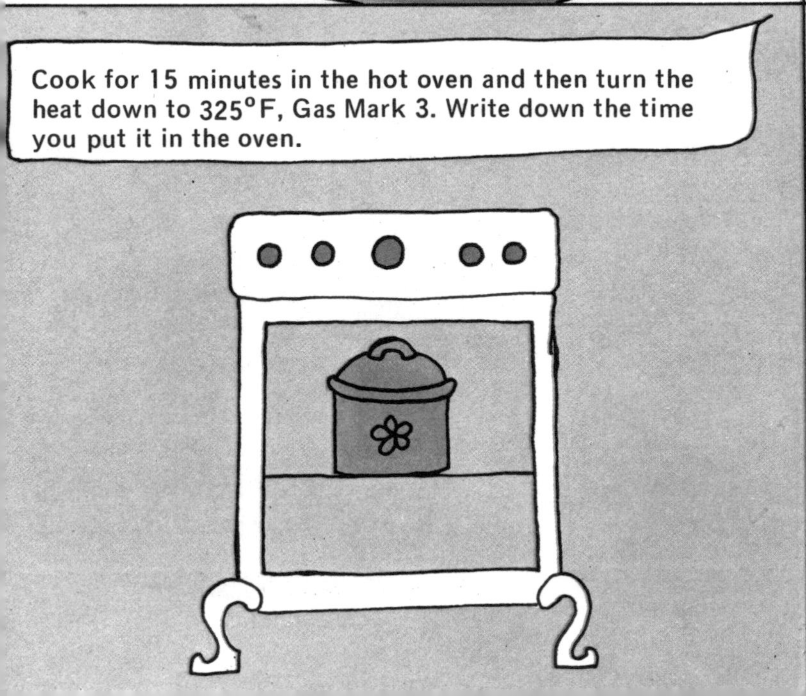
Cook for 15 minutes in the hot oven and then turn the heat down to 325°F, Gas Mark 3. Write down the time you put it in the oven.

It will be done after another 1½ hours. Serve with lots of mashed potatoes (page 39).
OVEN
OFF

Goulash

30

There are many different European countries which have their own goulash. This recipe comes from Hungary.

For 2 people you will need:

2 medium onions

½ green pepper (remove seeds)

1 carrot

2 ounces (4 tablespoons) of margarine

1 pound of lamb or beef

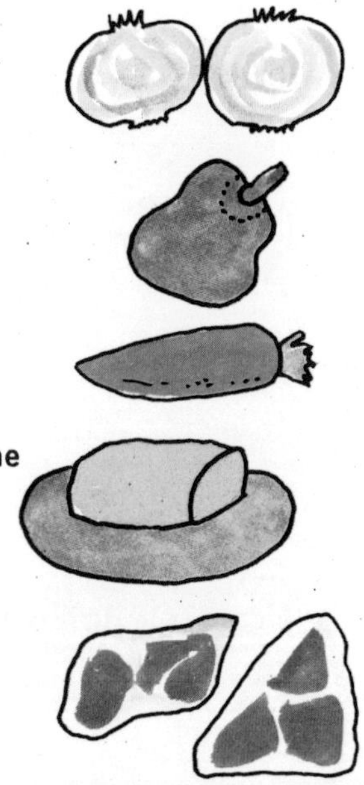

1 rounded tablespoon (1¼ tablespoons) of flour

¼ teaspoon of mixed dried herbs

½ rounded teaspoon of paprika

¼ teaspoon of salt

a pinch of cayenne pepper

1 tablespoon (1¼ tablespoons) of tomato paste or purée

a pinch of nutmeg

1 bouillon cube

and ½ pint (1¼ cups) of water

whipped or sour cream

ON OVEN
Set the oven at 350°F, Gas Mark 4. Chop the onions, green pepper and carrot and fry them very gently, using the margarine. Put them into the casserole when they are beginning to get soft. Sharp knife.

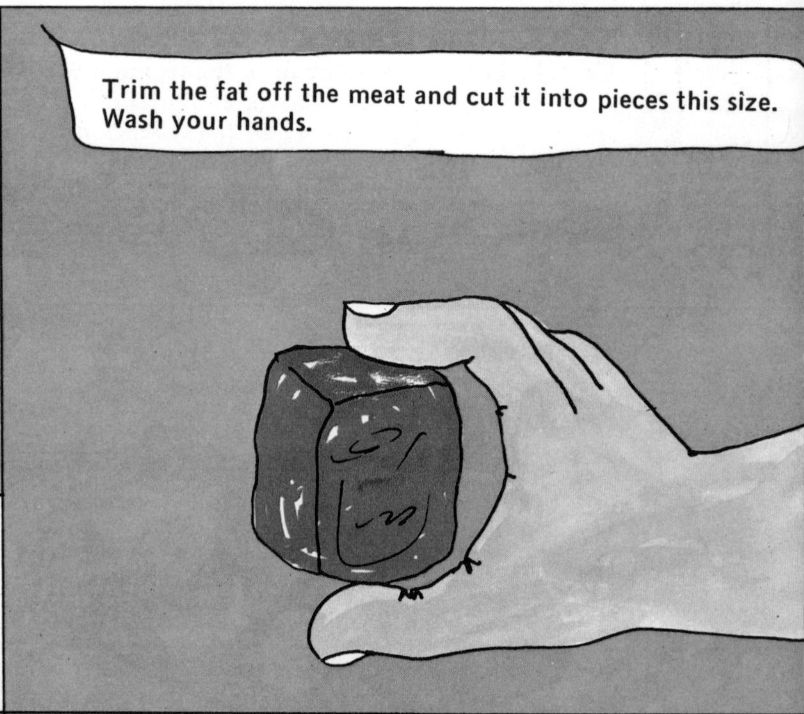
Trim the fat off the meat and cut it into pieces this size. Wash your hands.

Fry the meat on all sides in the frying pan. This is called 'sealing' the meat, because it keeps the juices from running out. You may have to use a little more margarine if the meat sticks.

Put the flour, herbs, paprika, salt, cayenne, tomato paste and nutmeg into the pan with the meat and stir. Turn off the heat.

1 sharp knife

1 chopping board

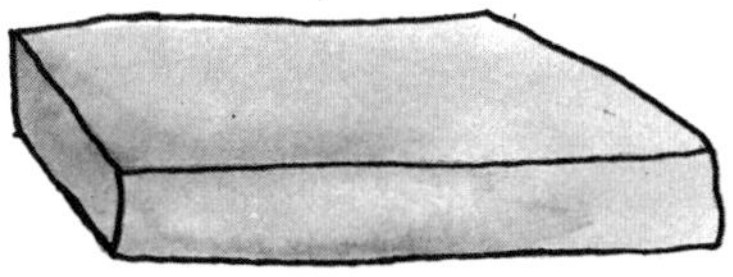

1 frying pan

1 casserole with lid

1 tablespoon

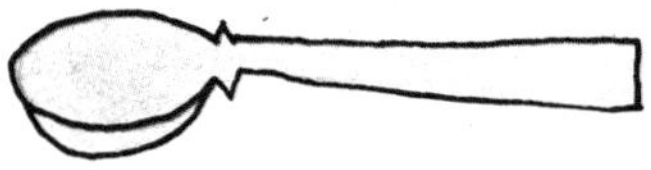

1 teaspoon

1 wooden spoon

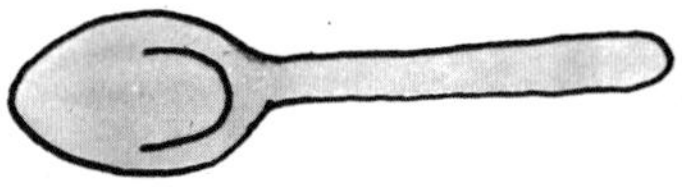

1 bowl

1 egg whisk (for cream)

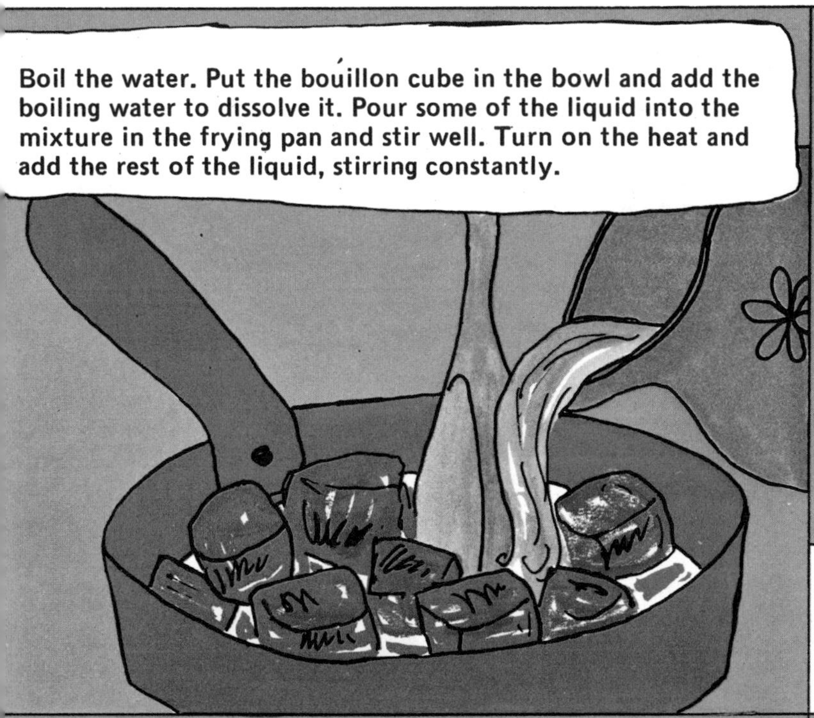
Boil the water. Put the bouillon cube in the bowl and add the boiling water to dissolve it. Pour some of the liquid into the mixture in the frying pan and stir well. Turn on the heat and add the rest of the liquid, stirring constantly.

Still stirring, bring the mixture to boiling point and then turn it into the casserole dish. Mix in the vegetables.

Place the lid on the casserole and put it into the oven for 2 hours. Write down the time you put it in.

Just before you serve it, pop a dollop of cream on top of the goulash. It's really great served with rice or mashed potatoes.
OVEN OFF

Pork in Sweet and Sour Sauce

Chinese children all love sweet and sour dishes — this is a variation of the food they might like to eat.

For 2 people you will need:

¾ pound of pork steak or lean pork

1 ounce (2 tablespoons) of margarine

1 onion

2 tomatoes

4 glace cherries

8 small pieces of tinned (canned) pineapple or 2 rings, cut up

¼ pint (½ cup + 3 tablespoons) of water, or pineapple juice

2 tablespoons (2½ tablespoons) of vinegar

¼ teaspoon of salt

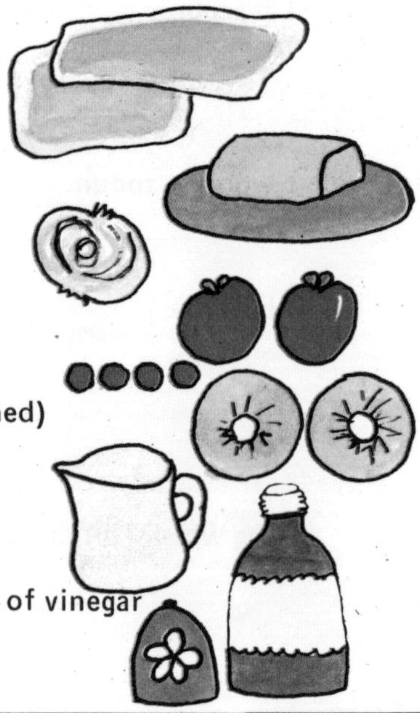

1 teaspoon of sugar

1 rounded tablespoon (1¼ tablespoons) of cornflour (cornstarch)

1 sharp knife

1 chopping board

1 frying pan

1 casserole dish

1 cup

1 tablespoon

1 teaspoon

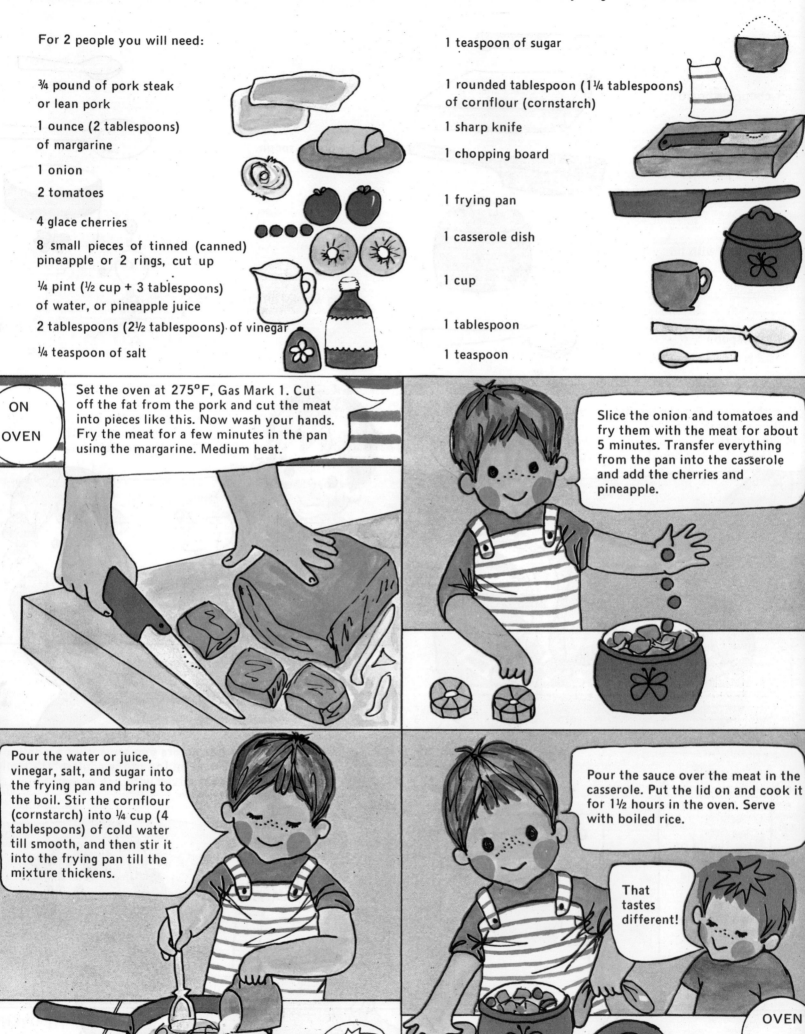

ON OVEN
Set the oven at 275°F, Gas Mark 1. Cut off the fat from the pork and cut the meat into pieces like this. Now wash your hands. Fry the meat for a few minutes in the pan using the margarine. Medium heat.
Slice the onion and tomatoes and fry them with the meat for about 5 minutes. Transfer everything from the pan into the casserole and add the cherries and pineapple.
Pour the water or juice, vinegar, salt, and sugar into the frying pan and bring to the boil. Stir the cornflour (cornstarch) into ¼ cup (4 tablespoons) of cold water till smooth, and then stir it into the frying pan till the mixture thickens.
Pour the sauce over the meat in the casserole. Put the lid on and cook it for 1½ hours in the oven. Serve with boiled rice.
That tastes different!
OVEN OFF

Spaghetti and Meat Balls

This recipe originated in Italy, but this is how American folk cook it.

For 3 people you will need:

1 small onion

3 tablespoons (3¾ tablespoons) of vegetable oil

1 16 ounce tin (can) of tomatoes

1 tablespoon (1¼ tablespoons) of tomato puree

1 teaspoon of salt

a shake of pepper

1 level teaspoon of paprika

2 teaspoons of Worcester sauce

¼ pound of raw spaghetti

2 slices of white bread

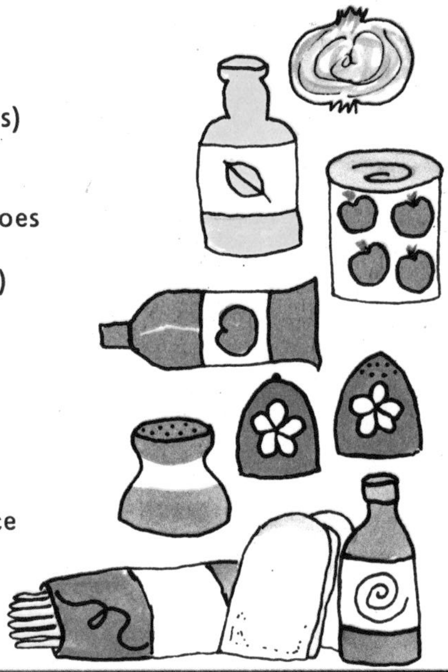

2 tablespoons (2½ tablespoons) of milk

½ pound of minced (ground) beef

1½ ounces (6 tablespoons) grated Parmesan cheese

1 knife

1 chopping board

2 frying pans

1 tablespoon

1 tin (can) opener

1 teaspoon

1 large saucepan with lid

1 fork

1 bowl

2

ON
OVEN
Set the oven at 200°F, Gas Mark ¼. Slice the onion and gently fry it for 5 minutes, using 1 tablespoon (1¼ tablespoons) of vegetable oil. Add the tomatoes, purée, ½ teaspoon of salt, pepper, paprika, Worcester sauce and about 2 tablespoons (2½ tablespoons) of water. Cook on a low heat for 15 minutes.
Cook the spaghetti as instructed on the packet (package) and leave it in the oven to keep warm.
Remove crusts and crumble the bread into a bowl with milk and ½ teaspoon of salt. Add the beef and mix well, using the fork. Form the mixture into 12 balls using your hands. Wash your hands.
Warm 2 tablespoons (2½ tablespoons) of the oil in the second frying pan and fry the meat balls for 10 minutes, on medium heat. Using the spoon, turn them occasionally and fry them until they are brown and crispy. Turn off the heat.
Add the meat balls to the sauce, stir, and cook for another 5 minutes. Make a spaghetti nest on each plate, place 4 meat balls in the centre of each nest, and spoon the sauce over.
Let your friends sprinkle Parmesan cheese over if they like it.
OVEN
OFF

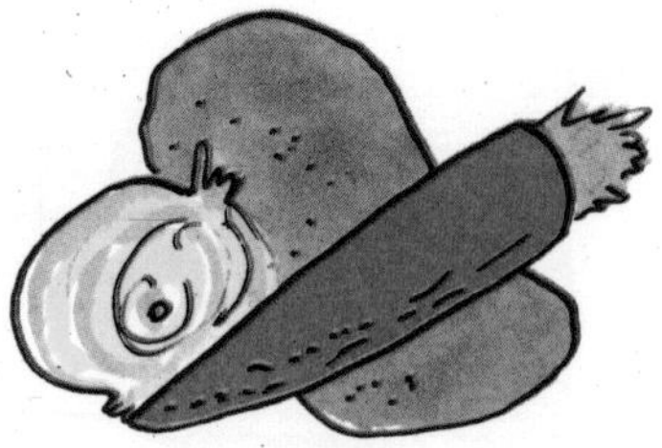

Vegetables are always much tastier and more nourishing if you do not overcook them. If you are boiling them, then you should save the water they are boiled in and use it as stock for gravy, soup or meat dishes in which you require stock.

White Sauce

A white sauce is the basis for a number of different sauces. It is essential for many recipes in this book. You may use it with vegetables like cauliflower or carrots, or pour it over fish. If you add 2 ounces (½ cup) of grated cheese you will have a cheese sauce. Add 2 tablespoons (2½ tablespoons) of tomato ketchup and you have a tomato sauce. You may experiment yourself.

For ½ pint (1¼ cups) you will need:

1 ounce (2 tablespoons) of butter

1 heaped tablespoon (1¼ tablespoons) of flour

a pinch of salt and a shake of pepper

½ pint (1¼ cups) of milk

1 small saucepan
1 tablespoon
1 wooden spoon
1 cup

you might need an egg whisk

Melt the butter in the pan on a low heat. Add the flour, salt and pepper and mix well with the wooden spoon. Heat off.

Still stirring!
Carefully add the milk a little at a time, stirring constantly to prevent any lumps from forming. Now turn the heat on. Bring the sauce to the boil.

Keep stirring! Boil for 5 minutes on a low heat. If it begins to go lumpy, turn off the heat and whisk it like crazy — then you can boil it up again.
You need not tell anyone you whisked it though!

Rice (for savoury dishes)

If you buy good quality rice, it is easy to cook it properly if you follow these instructions.
So many grown-ups have difficulty cooking rice — it would be fun for you to show them how!

For each person you will need:

1½ pints (3¾ cups) of water

1 teaspoon of salt

3 ounces (½ cup) of uncooked rice (long grain)

1 sieve

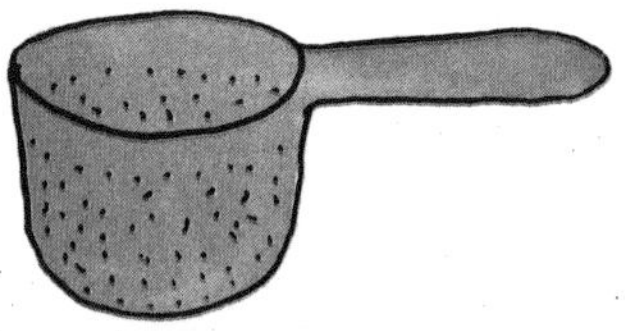

1 saucepan with lid

1 fork

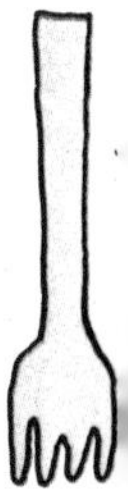

1 serving dish with lid

ON
OVEN
Set the oven at 300° F, Gas Mark 2. Place the rice in the sieve and rinse it under the cold water tap. Bring the water to the boil in the saucepan and add salt.
Add the rice and bring the water to boiling point, then cover the pan with the lid. Turn the heat to low.
After 11 minutes take a little of the rice on a fork, leave it to cool and then taste it. It should not be nutty. If it is, leave it for another 2 minutes and try again. Cook till firm but not too soft.
Do not overcook.
Pour the rice into the sieve, rinse it under cold water, place it in the serving dish and warm it in the oven for 20 minutes.
OVEN
OFF

Salads and French Dressing 36

You will find that salad will complement almost all meat, fish or cheese dishes. You can use many fresh raw vegetables and some cold cooked ones. One of the best ways to serve salad is to chop up the ingredients finely and coat them with a French dressing. Then you can serve the salad in individual bowls or in a large bowl lined with lettuce leaves. Here is an example.

For 2 people you will need:

¼ apple

a large slice of onion

2 tomatoes

¼ cucumber

8 lettuce leaves

1 sharp knife

1 chopping board

a salad bowl or two small bowls

For the French dressing you will need:

2 tablespoons (2½ tablespoons) of vinegar

4 tablespoons (5 tablespoons) of oil

½ teaspoon of castor sugar (superfine)

¼ teaspoon of salt

a few shakes of pepper (better if it's freshly ground black pepper)

a pinch of mustard powder

1 wide-necked bottle with top

1 teaspoon 1 tablespoon

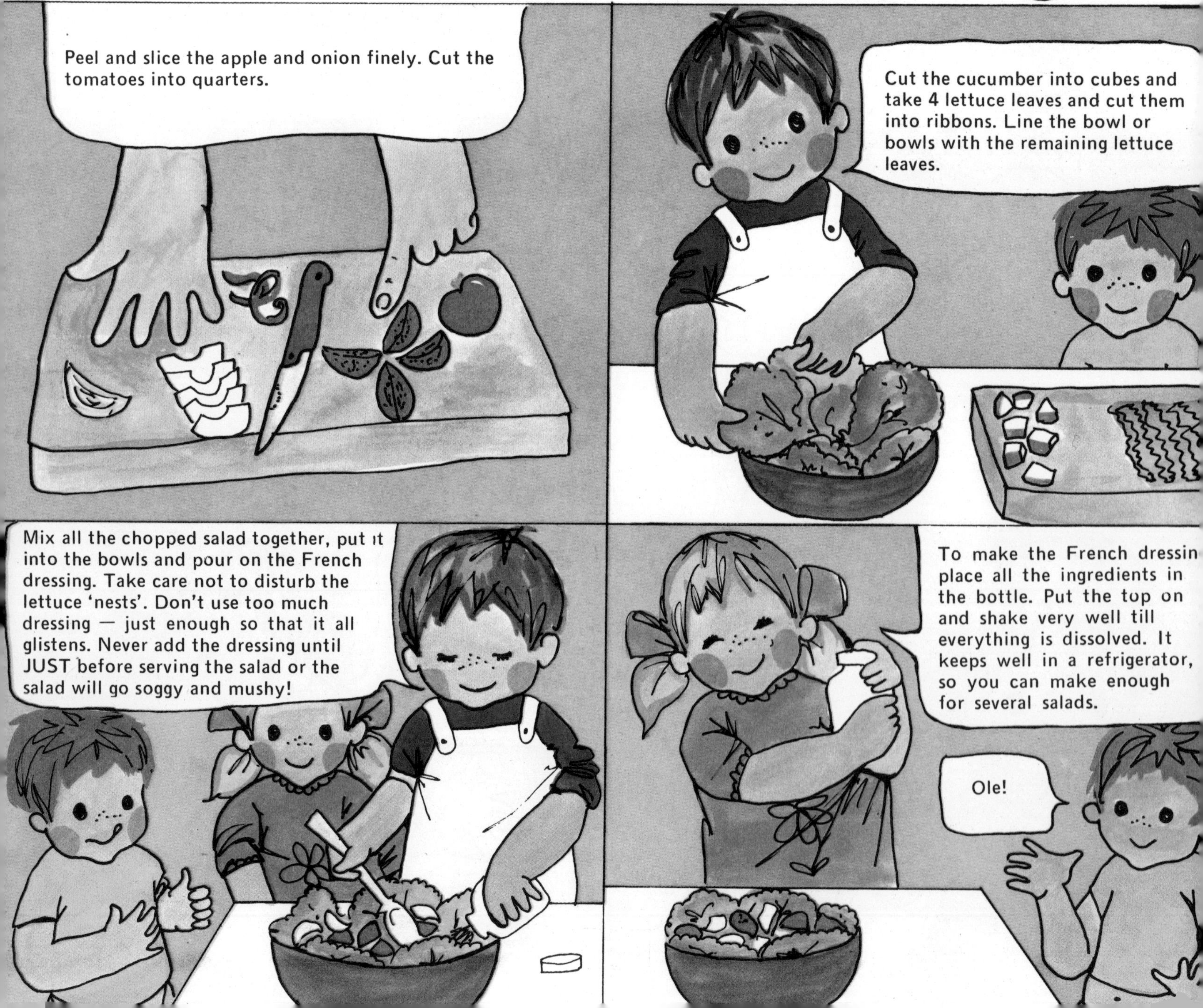

Peel and slice the apple and onion finely. Cut the tomatoes into quarters.
Cut the cucumber into cubes and take 4 lettuce leaves and cut them into ribbons. Line the bowl or bowls with the remaining lettuce leaves.
Mix all the chopped salad together, put it into the bowls and pour on the French dressing. Take care not to disturb the lettuce 'nests'. Don't use too much dressing — just enough so that it all glistens. Never add the dressing until JUST before serving the salad or the salad will go soggy and mushy!
To make the French dressin place all the ingredients in the bottle. Put the top on and shake very well till everything is dissolved. It keeps well in a refrigerator, so you can make enough for several salads.
Ole!

Waldorf Salad

This delicious salad comes from America. Children there love to mix sweet and sour flavours together. It is a colourful salad to make in the winter, when some vegetables for salad are difficult to find.

For enough for 4 people you will need:

3 red apples

4 sticks of celery

2 ounces (1/4 cup) of shelled walnuts

1/4 pint (1/2 cup) of mayonnaise or salad cream

6 lettuce leaves

1 grapefruit

1 large orange

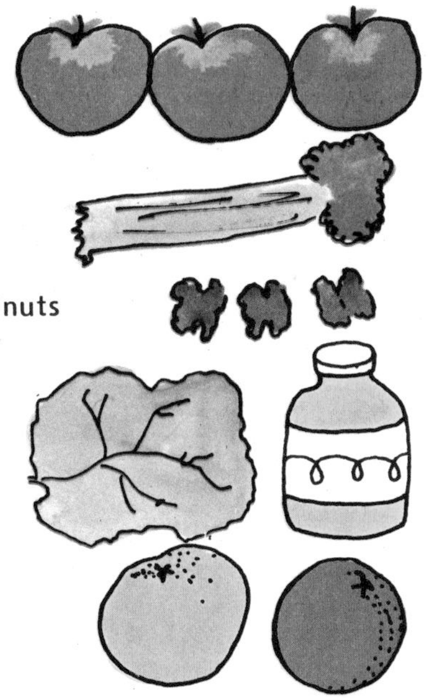

1 knife

1 chopping board

1 large bowl

1 tablespoon

1 large flat serving dish

Cut two of the apples into quarters and remove the cores. Chop each quarter into 3 or 4 neat pieces. Cut the celery into small strips. Place the apple and celery in the bowl.
Chop the walnuts into uneven pieces and put them into the bowl too. Pour over the mayonnaise or salad cream and mix well until everything is covered with the dressing.
Place the lettuce on the flat plate and put the mixture from the bowl into a neat pile in the centre of the lettuce.
Core and slice the remaining apple. Peel the orange and grapefruit and divide them into segments. Now decorate the dish by placing alternate pieces of each fruit around the edge. Place into the refrigerator for 2 hours.
That tastes super with just about any meal.

Vichy (Candied) Carrots

Vichy carrots originated in France. This is a very good way to make a plain vegetable exciting and special.

For 2 people you will need:

½ pound of carrots

2 ounces (4 tablespoons) of butter

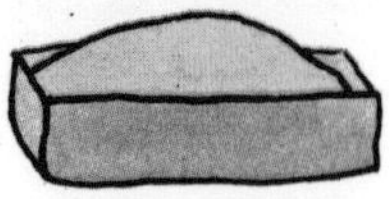

1 tablespoon (1¼ tablespoons) of water

2 teaspoons of granulated sugar

1 sharp knife

1 chopping board

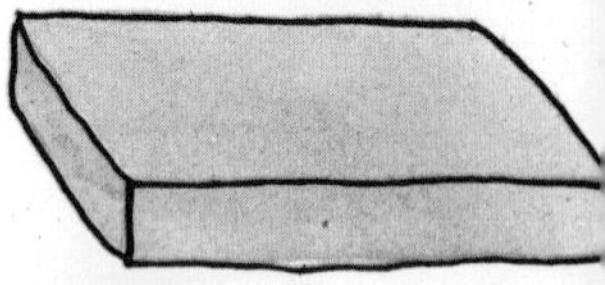

1 thick-bottomed saucepan with lid

1 tablespoon

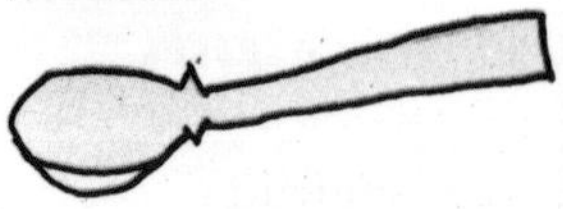

1 teaspoon

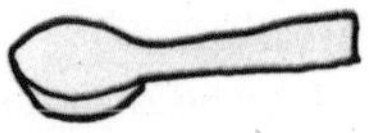

Wash and peel the carrots. Cut them in half. Then cut each half down the centre and then into thin strips.

Melt the butter in the pan and add the water and sugar.

Add the carrots and cover with the lid. Turn the heat very low. Cook for about an hour or until the carrots are soft.

Occasionally while they are cooking shake the pan so that the carrots do not stick to the bottom. When they are cooked, place them in a warm serving dish and eat with fish or meat.
Mmmmm!

Mashed Potatoes

Just about everybody loves mashed potatoes with their meat or fish.

For 2 people you will need:

2 potatoes (big ones if you are hungry)

½ level teaspoon of salt

1 tablespoon (1¼ tablespoons) of milk

2 teaspoons of butter

1 potato peeler

1 sharp knife

1 saucepan with lid

1 fork

1 sieve

1 potato masher or large fork

1 wooden spoon

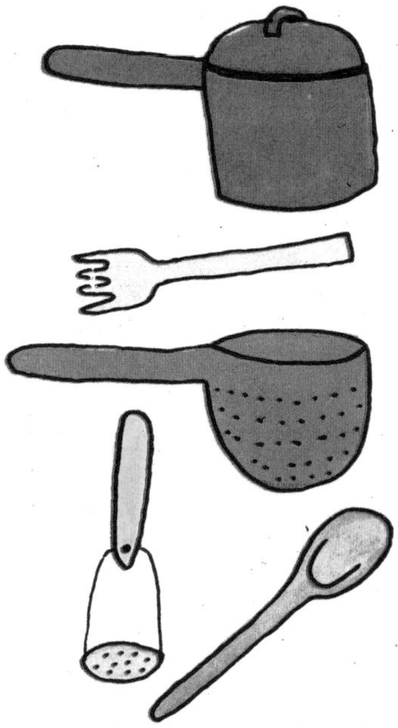

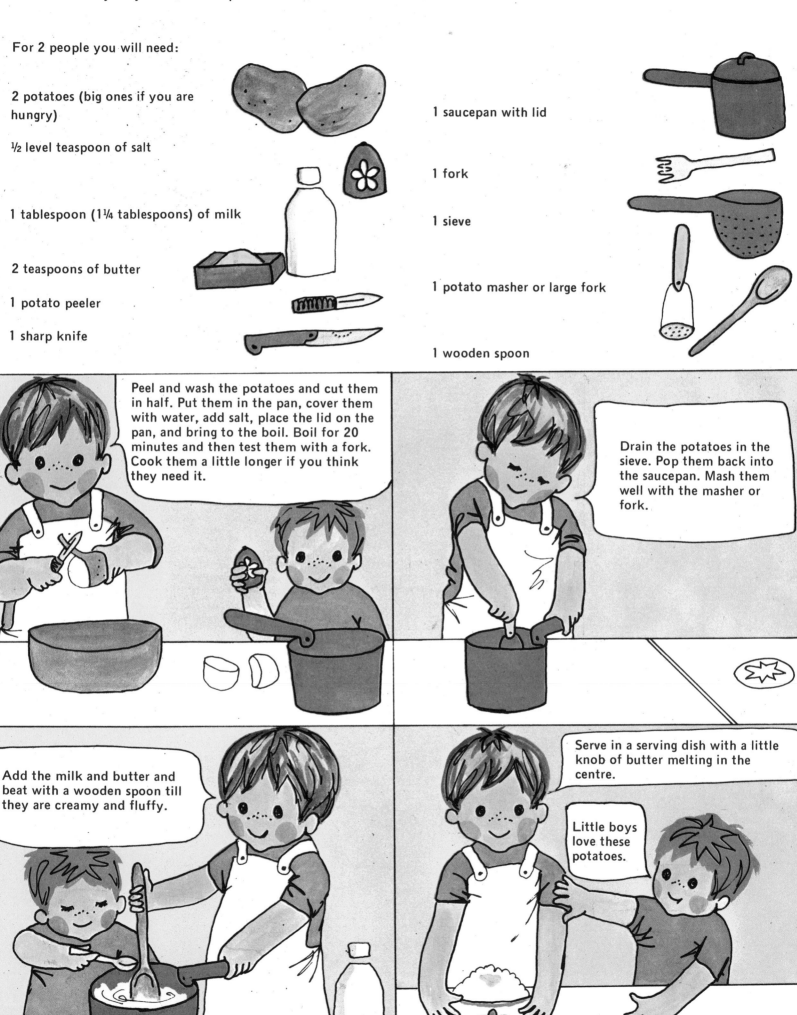

Peel and wash the potatoes and cut them in half. Put them in the pan, cover them with water, add salt, place the lid on the pan, and bring to the boil. Boil for 20 minutes and then test them with a fork. Cook them a little longer if you think they need it.
Drain the potatoes in the sieve. Pop them back into the saucepan. Mash them well with the masher or fork.
Add the milk and butter and beat with a wooden spoon till they are creamy and fluffy.
Serve in a serving dish with a little knob of butter melting in the centre.
Little boys love these potatoes.

Baked Potatoes

Eat baked potatoes with meat or fish. You can cook them in an open fire if you wrap them in foil. Serve with lots of butter.

For each person you will need:

1 large potato

1 tablespoon (1¼ tablespoons) of butter

1 scrubbing brush

1 knife

1 fork

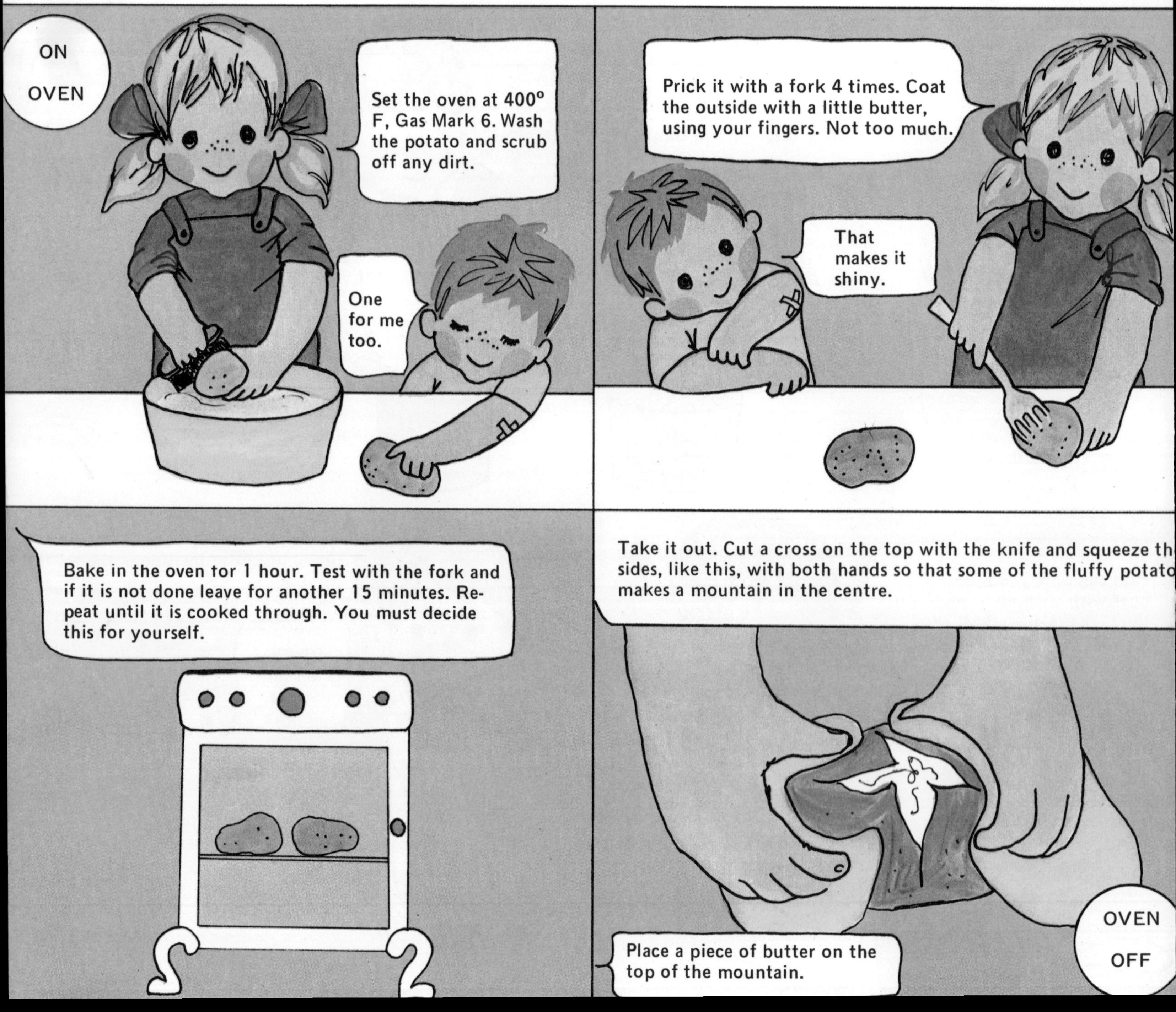
ON
OVEN
Set the oven at 400° F, Gas Mark 6. Wash the potato and scrub off any dirt.
One for me too.
Prick it with a fork 4 times. Coat the outside with a little butter, using your fingers. Not too much.
That makes it shiny.
Bake in the oven tor 1 hour. Test with the fork and if it is not done leave for another 15 minutes. Repeat until it is cooked through. You must decide this for yourself.
Take it out. Cut a cross on the top with the knife and squeeze th
sides, like this, with both hands so that some of the fluffy potato
makes a mountain in the centre.
Place a piece of butter on the top of the mountain.
OVEN
OFF

Potatoes and Onions

French children often have this with their roast meat or steak.

For 2 people you will need:

a little margarine

½ an onion

2 fairly large potatoes

a pinch of salt and a shake of pepper

½ pint (1¼ cups) of milk

a teaspoon of butter

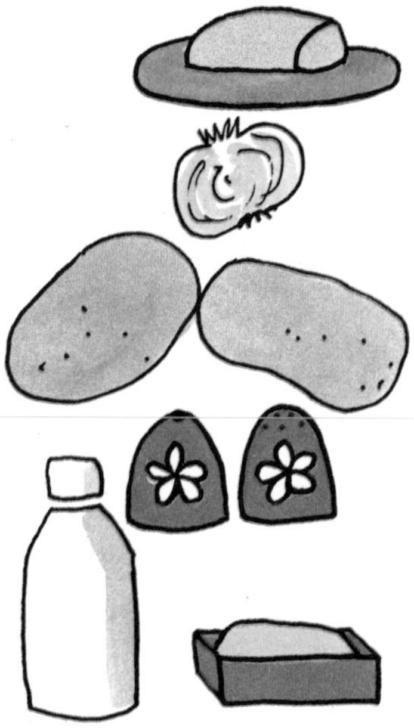

1 small ovenproof dish

1 knife

1 potato peeler

1 chopping board

1 small saucepan

1 teaspoon

ON OVEN
Set the oven at 350°F, Gas Mark 4. Grease the dish with the margarine. Peel the onion and wash and peel the potatoes.
Slice the potatoes into thin rounds. Chop the onion into small pieces.
Put alternate layers of potato and onion into the dish. Start and finish with a layer of potato.
Mix the salt and pepper with the milk and boil. Pour over the potatoes and place the butter on top. Bake in the oven for 1½ hours. Do not put a lid on the dish. The potatoes will be lovely and brown on top.
OVEN OFF

Potato Cakes

Sometimes your mother will have potatoes left over from a meal.
You can use these for the potato cakes, starting from the second picture.

For 8 cakes you will need:

½ pound of potatoes
(1 large or 2 small)

1 tablespoon (1¼ tablespoons)
of butter

½ level teaspoon of salt

2 ounces (½ cup) of flour

1 tablespoon (1¼ tablespoons)
of margarine

1 potato peeler

1 saucepan

1 fork

1 sieve

1 potato masher or large fork

1 wooden spoon

1 rolling pin

1 knife

1 frying pan

1 palette knife (spatula)

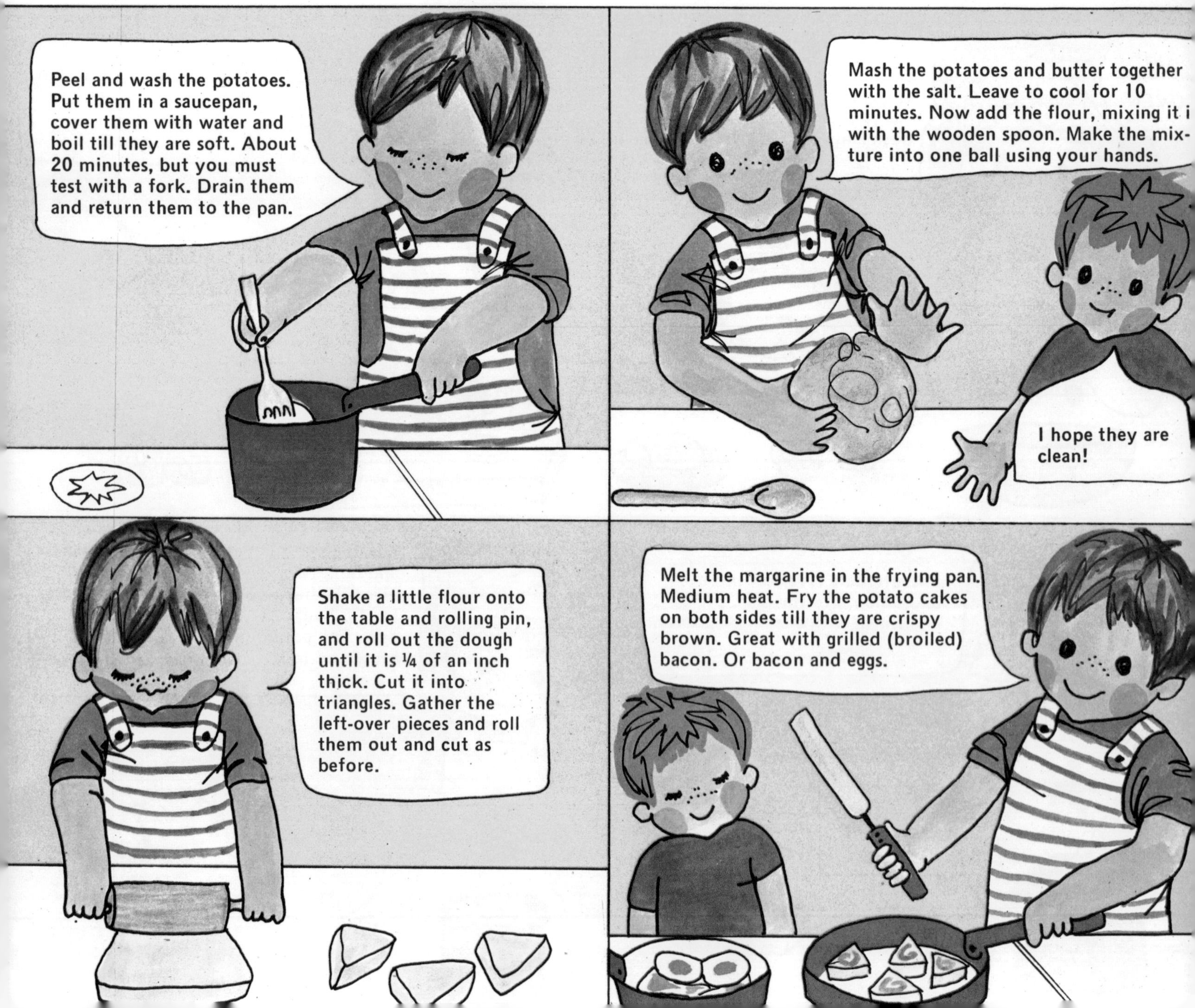

Peel and wash the potatoes. Put them in a saucepan, cover them with water and boil till they are soft. About 20 minutes, but you must test with a fork. Drain them and return them to the pan.
Mash the potatoes and butter together with the salt. Leave to cool for 10 minutes. Now add the flour, mixing it i with the wooden spoon. Make the mixture into one ball using your hands.
I hope they are clean!
Shake a little flour onto the table and rolling pin, and roll out the dough until it is ¼ of an inch thick. Cut it into triangles. Gather the left-over pieces and roll them out and cut as before.
Melt the margarine in the frying pan. Medium heat. Fry the potato cakes on both sides till they are crispy brown. Great with grilled (broiled) bacon. Or bacon and eggs.

Colcannon

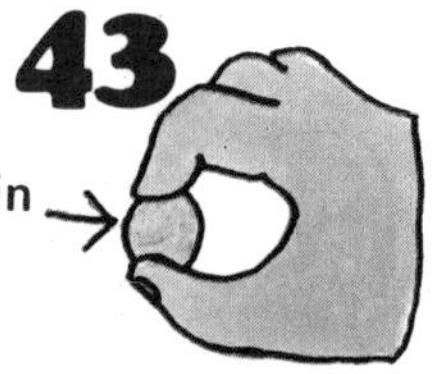
1 coin

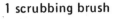

This recipe from Ireland is served for supper — most often at Hallowe'en. You can ask your dad to wrap a coin in foil and place it in the mixture. This brings luck to the finder.

For 4 people you will need:

1 pound of potatoes

1 pound of green cabbage

1 small onion

1 ounce (2 tablespoons) of butter

3 fluid ounces (½ cup) of milk

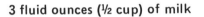

a pinch of salt and a shake of pepper

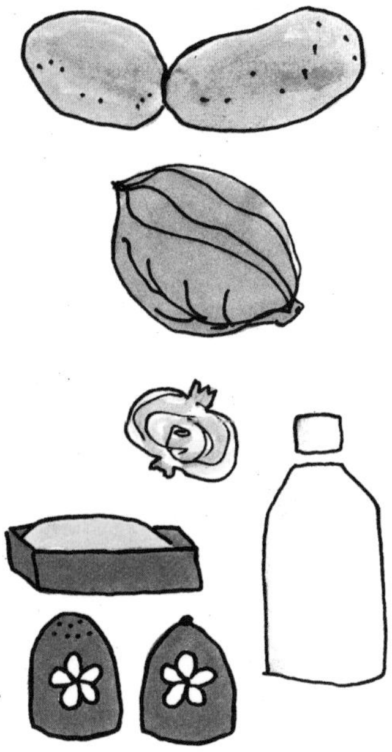

1 scrubbing brush

1 small saucepan with lid

1 fork

1 sieve

1 sharp knife

1 chopping board

1 large saucepan with lid

1 cup

1 potato masher

1 large serving plate

Scrub the potatoes, cover them with water and boil them in their jackets in the smaller saucepan. Test them with a fork after 20 minutes to see if they are cooked. Leave a little longer if they are not. Drain them into a sieve. Return them to the pan.

Take the cabbage leaves off and wash each one well. Peel and chop the onion. Place the cabbage and onion into the large saucepan with a cup of water, cover with the lid and bring to the boil. Lower the heat and cook till tender. Drain the cabbage in the sieve.

Remove the potato skins. Melt the butter slowly in a small saucepan.

Put the cabbage, onion, milk, salt, pepper and potatoes into the large saucepan and mash them well. It's hard work and finally should look like green mashed potato!

Arrange the mixture on the large plate, get your dad to hide the coin. Make a hole in the centre and pour in the melted butter. This is great with grilled (broiled) bacon or sausages.

The very best thing to eat after a meal is fresh fruit. Sometimes, though, you like to show how clever you are and make a dessert or pudding for a change.

Fried Bananas

You can make these even though you are quite small. If you are, make sure your mother is around.

For each person you will need:

1 banana

1 tablespoon (1¼ tablespoons) of flour

the pancake mixture on page 10, in a dish 1 tablespoon (1¼ tablespoons) of butter

a little castor sugar (superfine)

ice cream or whipped cream

1 knife

1 tablespoon

1 frying pan

1 fork

1 fish slice (spatula)

1 serving dish

Peel the banana and cut it in half. Then cut it in half again longways. It should look like this.
Dip each piece of banana into the flour and then into the pancake mixture — try making this with half the amount of milk. Then dip into the flour again.
Heat the butter in the frying pan till it is hot and then turn the heat down. Now fry the bananas till they are crispy and golden all over. Put them on a serving dish and sprinkle with castor sugar (superfine).
Serve immediately with the ice cream or whipped cream piled on top.
Smile at the compliments.

Orange Mousse

45

MAGIC!

The gravity defying dish! Your friends will wonder how you make this — you may not wish to tell! Start to prepare it 4 hours before you would like to eat it.

For 4 people you will need:

- a little butter for greasing
- ½ pint (1¼ cups) of water
- 1 packet of orange jelly (gelatin)
- ¼ pint (½ cup + 2 tablespoons) of evaporated milk
- 4 glacé cherries
- 2 squares of chocolate

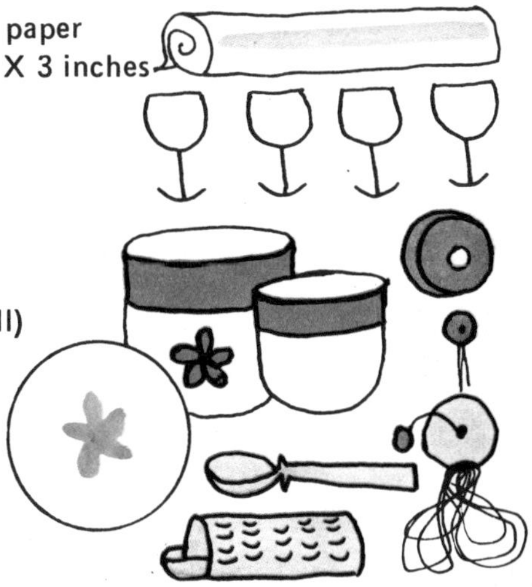

- 4 pieces of greaseproof paper (wax paper or foil), 11 X 3 inches
- 4 wine glasses
- adhesive tape
- 2 bowls (1 large, 1 small)
- 1 plate
- 1 egg whisk
- 1 tablespoon
- 1 grater

Grease the greaseproof paper (foil) with a little butter. Wrap it around the glasses to look like this. Secure the ends with tape and stick the paper to the glasses with the tape.

Boil the water. Place the jelly (gelatin) in the small bowl and pour the boiling water over it. Stir till dissolved. Cover with the plate and leave it in the refrigerator or a cool place to get cold but not set. This takes about an hour.

Beat the evaporated milk in the large bowl. It should be thick like whipped cream. Now pour the cold jelly into the large bowl and whisk or beat like crazy!
Your friend could hold the bowl and you could then work faster. It should be light and fluffy.

Spoon the mixture into the prepared glasses. Allow it to rise above the rim of the glass but not above the paper (foil) of course! Leave it in the refrigerator or a cool place to set. Remove paper (foil) when firm, very carefully. Decorate with a cherry and grated chocolate.

Lemon Fondant Sweets (Candies)

If you have a friend who has been ill, this would be a very good gift.
It is most important to make sure your hands are especially clean.

For 24 sweets you will need:

8 ounces (1⅔ cups) of icing (confectioner's) sugar

2 tablespoons (2½ tablespoons) of thick concentrated lemon squash

½ teaspoon of yellow colouring

12 glace cherries or 24 silver balls

a little extra icing sugar

1 bowl

1 tablespoon

1 teaspoon

1 wooden spoon

1 chopping board

1 rolling pin

1 knife

1 plate

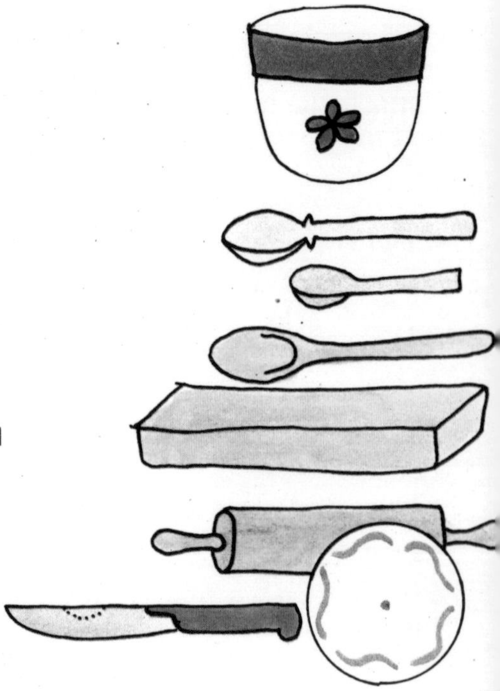

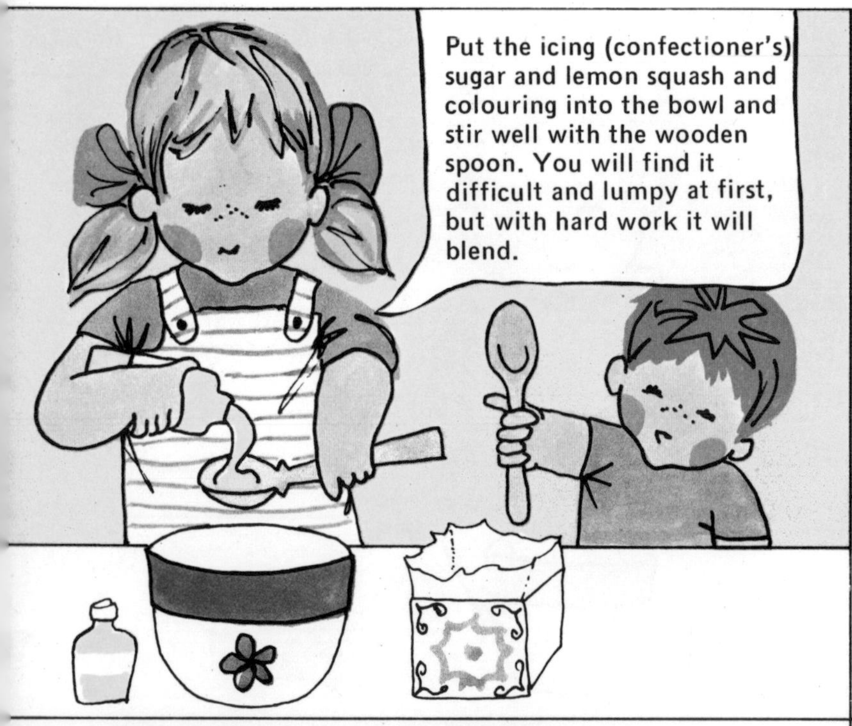
Put the icing (confectioner's) sugar and lemon squash and colouring into the bowl and stir well with the wooden spoon. You will find it difficult and lumpy at first, but with hard work it will blend.

Work the mixture together into one round ball. You may use your two clean hands.
I'll help if you like.

Sprinkle a little icing (confectioner's) sugar onto the board and the rolling pin and roll out the dough until it is about ¼ of an inch thick. Cut into 24 even-sized pieces.

Take each piece and roll it into a ball using your hands. Roll each ball into a little icing sugar and press it slightly flat. Place onto the plate and put half a cherry or one silver ball on each sweet. Leave to dry overnight.
Your mother mig help you to put them into a prett box for your frie

American Apple Pie

This delicious pie is very popular and is best served with ice cream, whipped cream or Cheddar cheese (American cheese). Eat it hot. I bet you won't be able to wait until it is cold anyway!

For one big pie with 6 to 8 slices, you will need:

1½ pounds of apples

a little margarine to grease the dish

the pastry on page 60 or 61

a little flour for rolling out

3 ounces (scant ½ cup) of sugar

½ teaspoon of cinnamon

1 tablespoon (1¼ tablespoons) of thick cream

½ ounce (1 tablespoon) of butter

enough milk to coat top of pie

1 sharp knife

1 pie dish about 9 or 10 inches across

1 rolling pin

1 teaspoon

1 tablespoon

1 fork

1 pastry brush or ball of cotton wool (cotton)

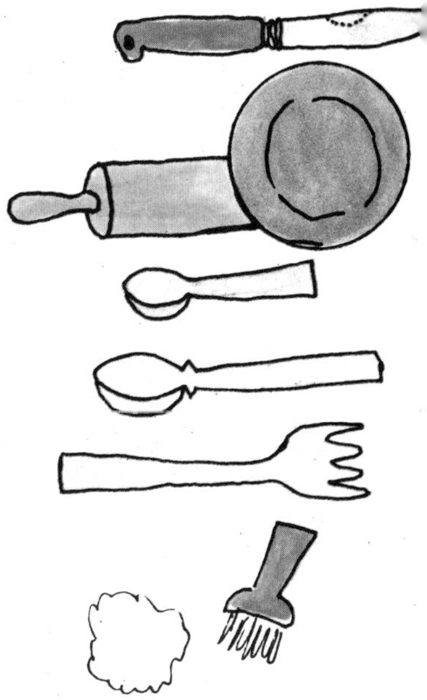

ON OVEN
Set the oven at 400°F, Gas Mark 6. Peel, core and slice the apples finely. Take care with that sharp knife. Grease the pie dish.
Divide the dough in half and work it into two very round even balls. Roll each out, using some extra flour. They must be ½ an inch larger than the pie dish. Place one in the dish.
rrange the apples eatly in a circle, arting at the centre, within an inch of e edge. Like this. se ⅓ of the apples. prinkle ⅓ of the gar and cinnamon ver the apples. Re-eat twice more ntil you have a ountain f apples.
Pour the cream over the centre and dot the butter over the last layer. Place the top dough over and dab a little water around the edge of the pastry so that the top will stick to it. Press the edges of the pie together with a fork. Prick a design on the top with the fork.
Paint the top with a little milk, using the pastry brush or cotton wool. Bake for 45 minutes.
Now that is really great!
OVEN OFF

Your Favourite Fruit Kuchen

Children in Germany really enjoy Kuchen on a winter evening. Sometimes they eat it cold with their tea. You can use your favourite tinned (canned) fruit for it — plums, gooseberries, apricots, peaches or cherries are best.

For a Kuchen large enough for 6 people you will need:

a little margarine for greasing the tin (pan)

2 large eggs

4 ounces (1 cup) of plain flour

½ level teaspoon of baking powder

1 ounce (2 tablespoons) of granulated sugar

¼ teaspoon of cinnamon

1½ ounces (3 tablespoons) of butter

8 drops of lemon essence (extract)

2 ounces (¼ cup) of castor sugar (superfine)

2 ounces (½ cup) of almonds

1 tin (can) of fruit, about 16 ounces

a little extra flour

a little whipped cream for decorating

ON OVEN
Set the oven at 450°F, Gas Mark 8. Grease the cake tin (pan). Separate the yolks and whites of eggs, as shown on page 4, and leave them aside in the cup and bowl.

Put the flour, baking powder, granulated sugar and cinnamon into the mixing bowl and stir.

Add the egg yolks, butter and lemon essence (extract) and mix with the wooden spoon. Work the mixture together until you have a dough.
It takes a bit of hard work mixing!

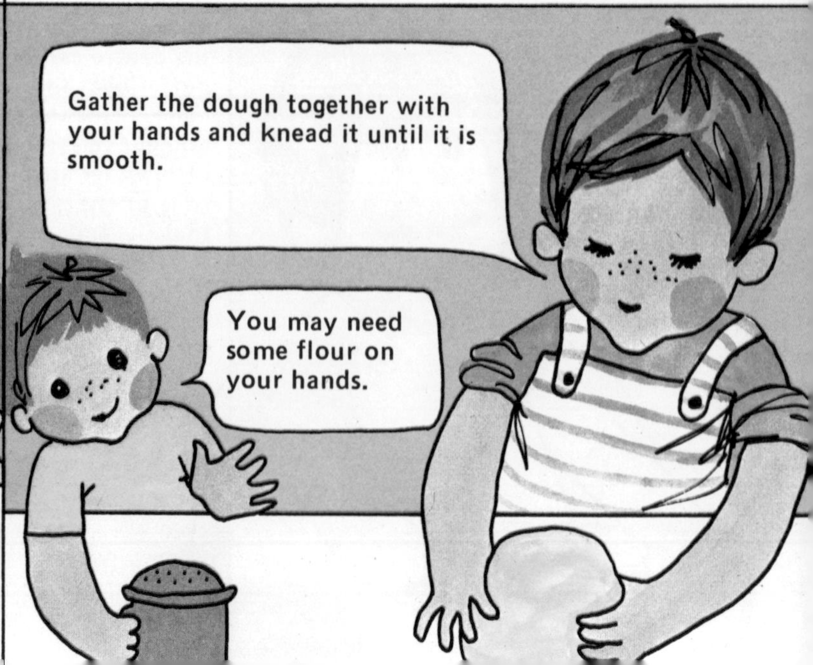
Gather the dough together with your hands and knead it until it is smooth.
You may need some flour on your hands.

1 cake tin (layer cake pan) 7 inches across

1 cup

1 bowl

1 large mixing bowl

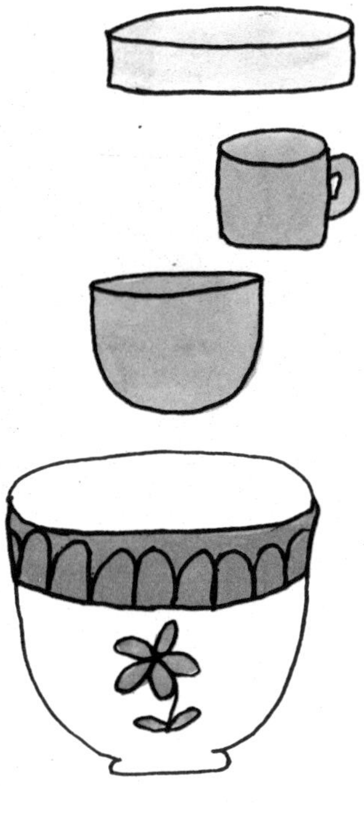

1 teaspoon

1 wooden spoon

1 rolling pin

1 egg whisk

1 tablespoon

1 can opener

1 sieve

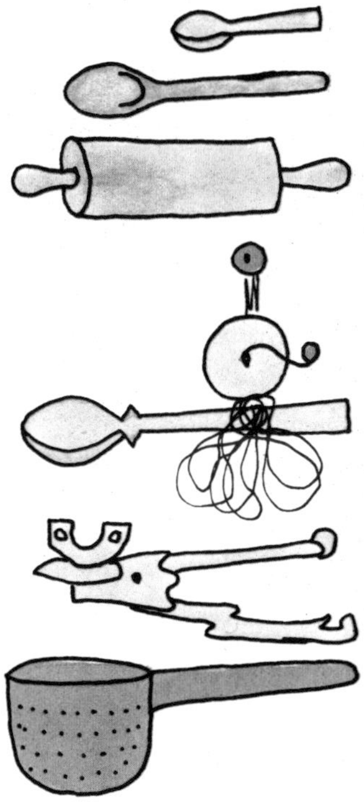

Make the dough into a ball. Sprinkle some flour on the table and rolling pin, and roll the dough out into a circle to fit the cake tin (pan) exactly. You will now put the dough into the tin (pan).

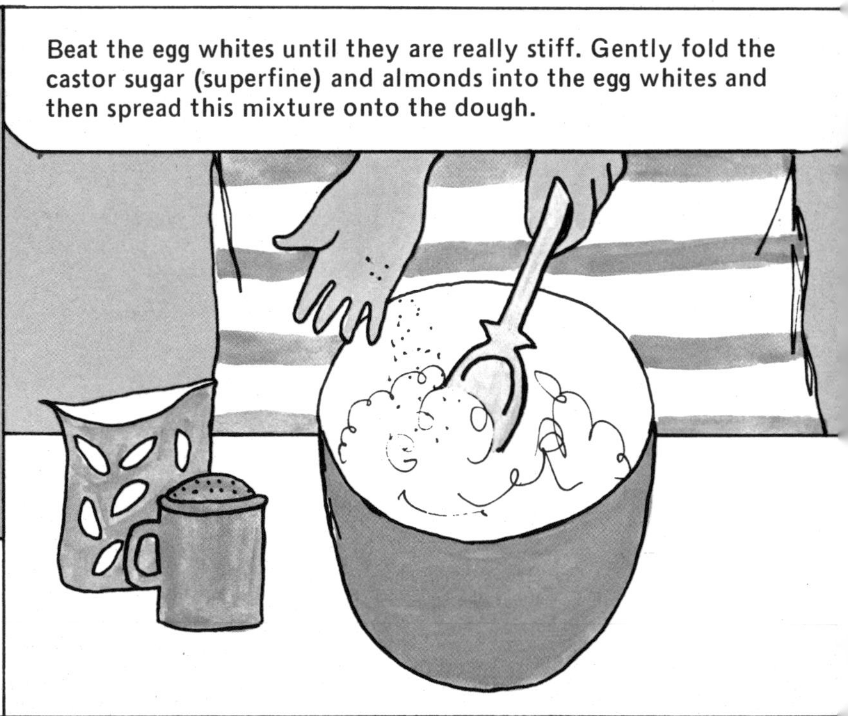
Beat the egg whites until they are really stiff. Gently fold the castor sugar (superfine) and almonds into the egg whites and then spread this mixture onto the dough.

Using the sieve, drain the juice from the fruit. Spoon the fruit gently onto the egg white mixture taking care not to break the fruit.
I know that's going to be super!

Place it in the oven. Write down the time you put it in and after 10 minutes turn the heat down to 350°F, Gas Mark 4. Cook it for another 45 minutes and then decorate with whipped cream when you serve it.
You will deserve the grateful thanks of your friends for your effort in making this delicious kuchen.
OVEN
OFF

Baking is great fun — but you must follow the instructions accurately or the bake will not turn out as you expect. It is most important to measure the ingredients exactly. You might like to do one or two of these recipes next time you're having a birthday party. Never open the oven before the baking is finished — you might spoil it.

Scotch Krispies

Big and little brothers will love these at tea-time.

For 10 krispies you will need:

1 ounce (¼ cup) of plain flour
4 ounces (1 cup) of uncooked porridge oats (oatmeal)
a pinch of salt
½ teaspoon of baking powder
2 ounces (4 tablespoons) of margarine
2 ounces (¼ cup) of sugar

a little extra margarine
1 tablespoon (1¼ tablespoons) of golden syrup (dark corn syrup)
1 bowl
1 tablespoon
1 wooden spoon
1 saucepan
1 small baking tin (pan)
1 knife

ON OVEN
Set the oven at 375° F, Gas Mark 5. Put the flour, porridge (oatmeal), salt and baking powder into the bowl. Mix.
Put the margarine, sugar and syrup into the saucepan. Heat until the mixture is melted, low heat.
Now pour the contents of the saucepans into the bowl. Mix really well with the wooden spoon. You may use your hands to get the mixture together.
Grease the baking tin (pan) with the extra margarine. Press the mixture into the tin (pan) making sure the top is flat and even.
Bake in the centre of the oven for 45 minutes. Write down the time you put it in. Cut into squares whe it is cool.
OVE OFF

Melting Lemon or Chocolate Drops

They don't need to be chewed — they just melt in your mouth. They are very good for little people who enjoy eating but like to be lazy. Great for tea parties!

For 12 cookies you will need:

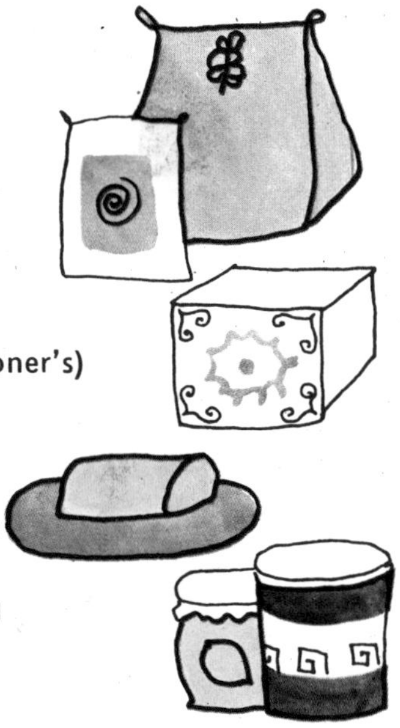

2 ounces (1/2 cup) of plain flour

2 ounces (1/2 cup) of cornflour (cornstarch)

1 ounce (1/4 cup) of icing (confectioner's) sugar

4 ounces (1/2 cup) of soft margarine

a little extra margarine for greasing

lemon curd (lemon cream) or chocolate spread

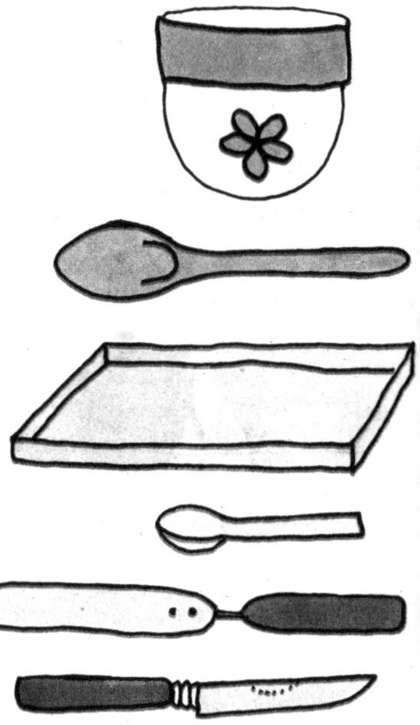

1 bowl

1 wooden spoon

1 large baking tin (cooky sheet)

1 teaspoon

1 palette knife (spatula)

1 knife

ON OVEN
Set the oven at 375°F, Gas Mark 5. Place the flour, cornflour (cornstarch), sugar and margarine into the bowl and stir well with the wooden spoon to get the mixture together. Mix until it is smooth.

Grease the baking tin (cooky sheet) with margarine. Put one teaspoon of the mixture into the tin (sheet) at a time, using your fingers to push it off the spoon. Space the cookies well apart — they spread as they cook. You should have 24 dollops.

Bake in the centre of the oven for 20 minutes. When they are cold remove them from the tin (sheet) by lifting them gently with a palette knife.
They are very delicate so treat them with great respect.

Matching cookies the same size, carefully sandwich them together with the lemon curd (cream) or chocolate spread.
I know someone who will help you to eat them.
OVEN OFF

Semolina Shortbread Cookies

People who like cookies will appreciate these.

For 30 cookies you will need:

a little margarine for greasing

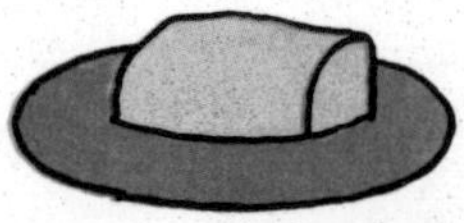

6 ounces (¾ cup) of butter

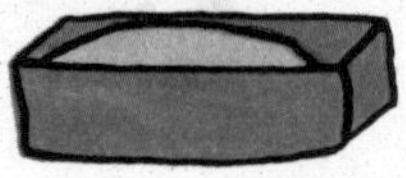

4 ounces (½ cup) of sugar

4 ounces (1 cup) of semolina (Cream of Wheat)

4 ounces (1 cup) of plain flour

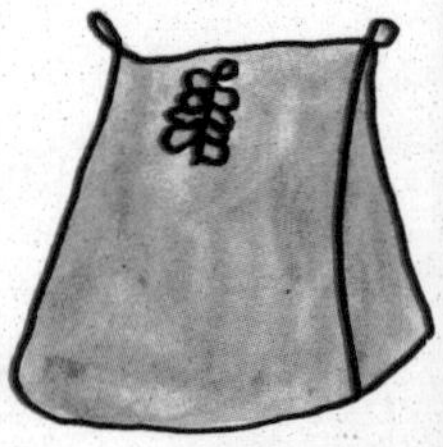

a little flour for rolling

15 glacé cherries

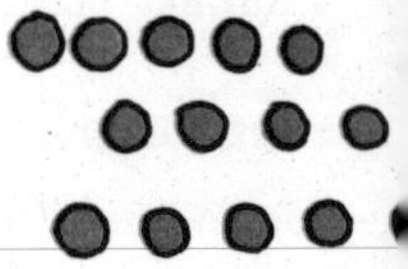

ON OVEN
Set the oven at 350° F, Gas Mark 4. Grease the 2 baking trays (sheets) with the margarine.

Mix the butter and sugar until they are smooth, using the larg bowl. Place the semolina and flour in the small bowl.

Gradually add the contents of the small bowl to the large one, stirring all the time. It is hard work but worth it!

Use your hands to make the ingredients into one big ball. Knead it together as you would plasticine.
That looks fun!

2 large baking trays
(cooky sheets)

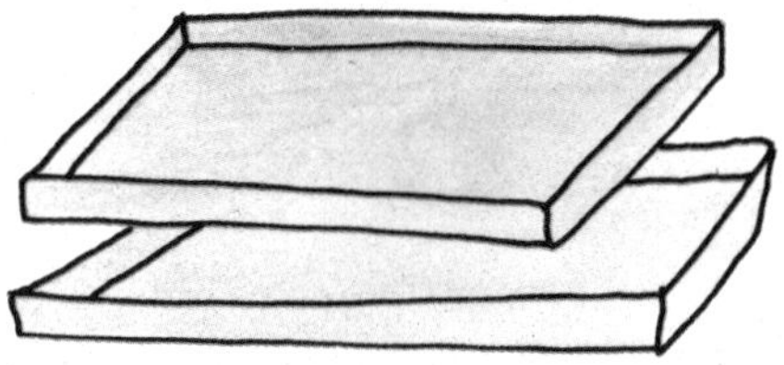

1 large bowl

a wooden spoon

1 small bowl

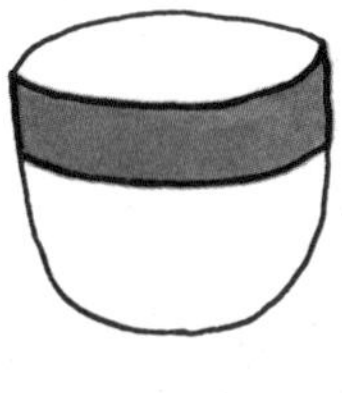

a rolling pin

a biscuit cutter or glass

a fish slice (spatula)

Sprinkle a little flour onto the table and rolling pin and roll the dough until it is as thin as a biscuit.
Cut the shapes with the cutter or glass. Gather the pieces left over, press them together and roll out again. Cut as before and repeat until all the dough is used.
Place the cookies on the baking trays (sheets) and press half a cherry on the centre of each cookie.
Bake in the centre of the oven for 20 minutes. Remember to write down the time you put them in. Leave them to cool and then ease off each cookie with a palette knife (spatula).
Oh boy!
OVEN
OFF

Raisin Scones

Raisin scones are always welcome at tea-time.

For 8 scones you will need:

8 ounces (2 cups) of plain flour

¼ teaspoon of salt

2½ rounded teaspoons (2¾ teaspoons) of baking powder

1½ ounces (1¾ tablespoons) of sugar

1½ ounces (3 tablespoons) of butter or margarine

2 ounces (½ cup) of raisins

3 fluid ounces (¼ cup + 1 tablespoon) of milk

a little extra flour

1 mixing bowl

1 teaspoon

1 fork

1 baking tray (cooky sheet)

1 knife

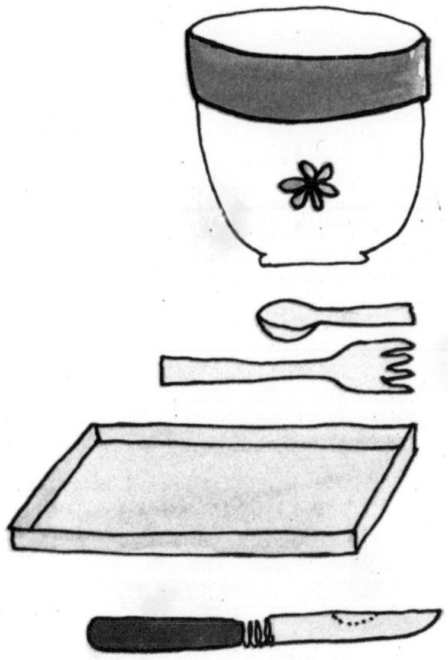

ON OVEN
Set the oven at 450°F, Gas Mark 8. Place the flour, salt, baking powder and sugar in the bowl. Rub in the butter or margarine with your fingers.
Mix in the raisins. Stir. Mix in the milk with the fork until you have the dough together. You may nee a very little more milk to make th dough more manageable.
You may use your hands.
Sprinkle the table with flour, turn out the dough, and make it into a round. Sprinkle it with flour, knead it lightly with the tips of your fingers and flatten it with the palm of your hand. It should be about ½ an inch thick.
Shake a little flour onto the baking tray (sheet).
Nearly ready for the oven.
Cut the dough into 8 triangles and arrange them on the tray (sheet). Leave plenty of room between eac one. Cook in the oven for 10 minutes. Eat some hot with butter.
Oh boy! Share them with your pals.
OVEN OFF

Chocolate Kisses

Your friends will like these when they come to see you. If you make them for your family, perhaps they will let you share some of them.

For 15 cookies you will need:

6 ounces (1½ cups) of plain flour

1 rounded teaspoon (1½ teaspoons) of baking powder

2 ounces (½ cup) of drinking chocolate powder

4 ounces (½ cup) of soft margarine

3 ounces (½ cup) of sugar

1 egg

a little margarine to grease the trays

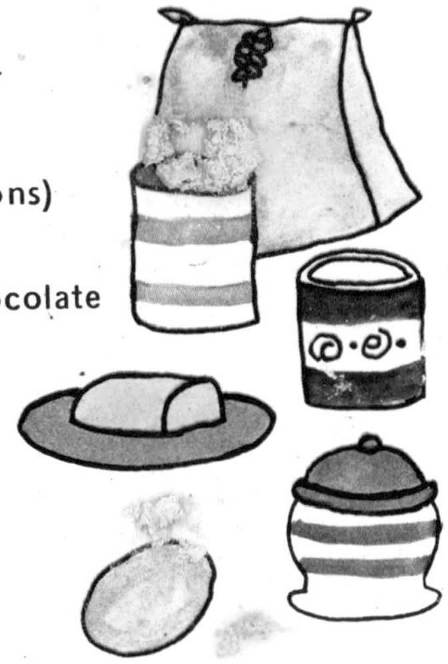

For the filling:

the butter icing (frosting) on page 57

1 large mixing bowl

1 wooden spoon

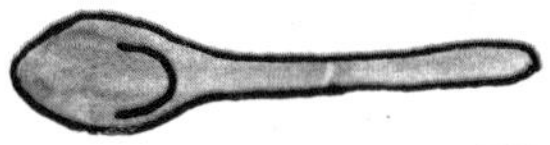

2 baking trays (cooky sheets)

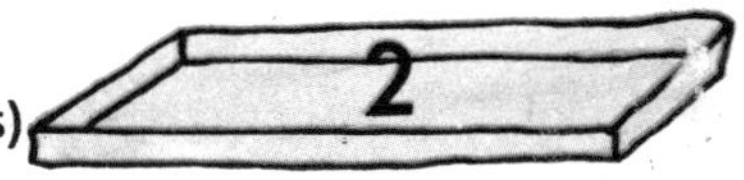
2

1 teaspoon

1 palette knife (spatula)

ON
OVEN
Set the oven at 325°F, Gas Mark 3. Place all the ingredients in the bowl.
Mix well with the wooden spoon. Use your hands to get the mixture into one big ball.
I'll help.
Grease the baking trays (sheets) well. Put 1 teaspoon of the mixture onto the tray (sheet), using your finger to push it off the spoon. Continue until you have 15 on each tray (sheet), spaced well apart.
Bake in the centre of the oven for 25 minutes. Write down the time when you put them in. When they are cool, ease them off the trays (sheets) carefully. Stick them together in pairs with the icing (frosting) on page 57.
OVEN
OFF

Chocolate Surprise Cake

You could make this for a real surprise. There is enough for 6 or 8 people.

You will need:

6 ounces (1½ cups) of plain flour

6 ounces (¾ cup) of soft margarine

6 ounces (¾ cup) of sugar

3 eggs

1 heaped teaspoon (1¼ teaspoons) of baking powder

a little extra margarine for greasing

1 small packet of chocolate buttons (bits)

1 mixing bowl

1 sieve

1 wooden spoon

1 teaspoon

2 rounds of greaseproof paper (wax paper or foil) to fit the bottom of the tins

2 sponge cake tins (pans), about 7 inches across

1 knife

1 wire rack

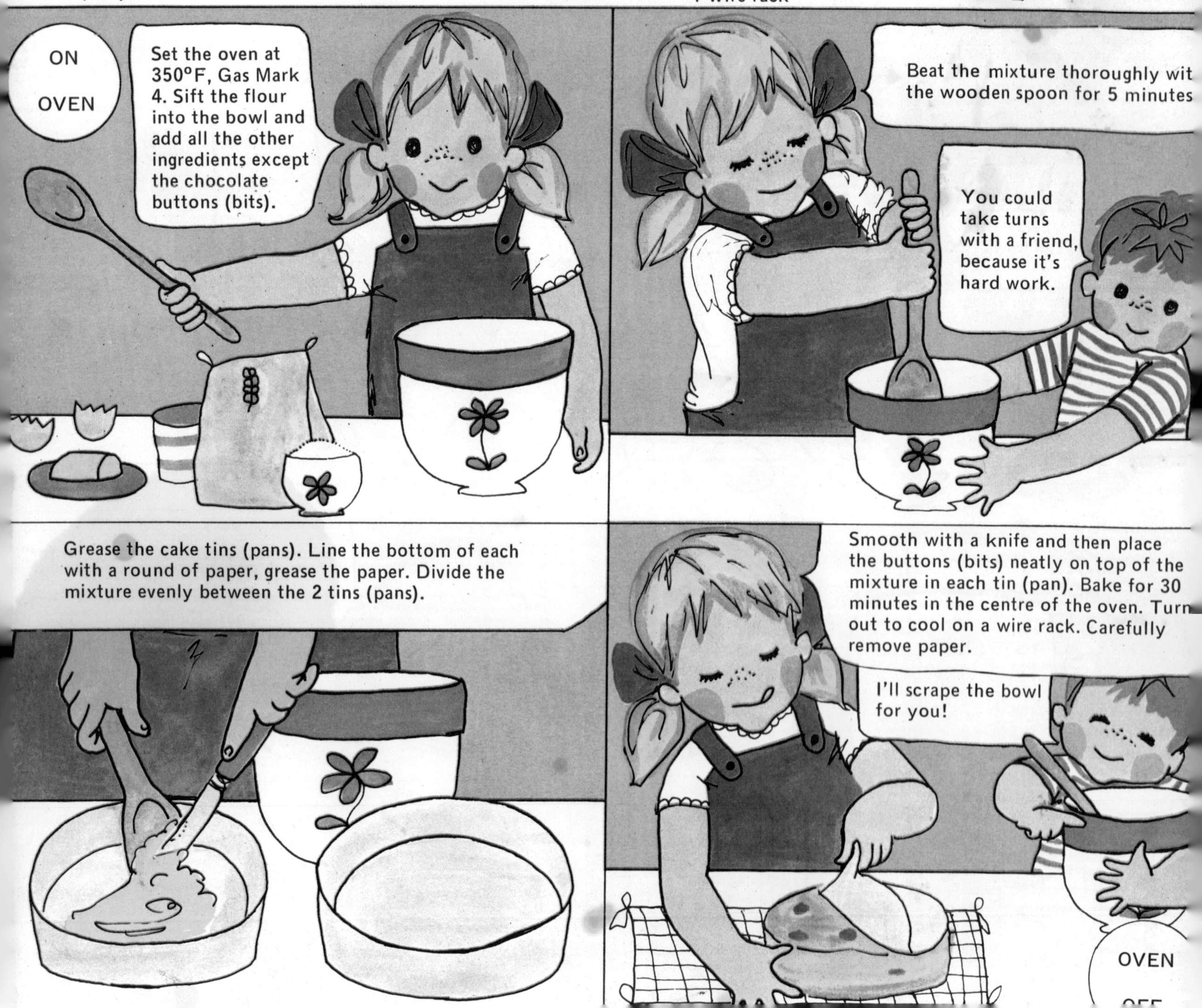
ON OVEN
Set the oven at 350°F, Gas Mark 4. Sift the flour into the bowl and add all the other ingredients except the chocolate buttons (bits).
Beat the mixture thoroughly wit the wooden spoon for 5 minutes
You could take turns with a friend, because it's hard work.
Grease the cake tins (pans). Line the bottom of each with a round of paper, grease the paper. Divide the mixture evenly between the 2 tins (pans).
Smooth with a knife and then place the buttons (bits) neatly on top of the mixture in each tin (pan). Bake for 30 minutes in the centre of the oven. Turn out to cool on a wire rack. Carefully remove paper.
I'll scrape the bowl for you!
OVEN

Chocolate Butter Icing (Frosting)

This is how you can finish the cake on page 56. You will need the last third of the chocolate buttons (bits) too.

You will need:

4 ounces (8 tablespoons) of soft margarine

4 ounces (3/4 cup) of icing (confectioner's) sugar

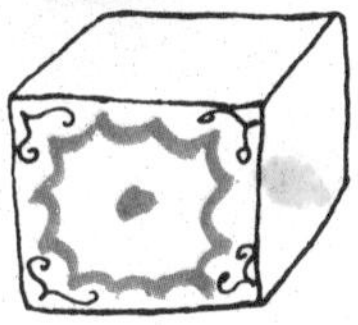

4 ounces (1/2 cup) of powdered drinking chocolate (cocoa)

1 tablespoon (1 1/4 tablespoons) of concentrated orange juice

1 mixing bowl

1 tablespoon

1 wooden spoon

1 knife

Put all the ingredients into the mixing bowl and stir. When they are blended, beat them well with the wooden spoon.
Turn the cakes to right side up. Spread the top of each cake with the butter icing.
Now put one cake on top of the other. That looks good.
May I scrape the bowl?
Decorate with the remaining chocolate buttons (bits).

Lazy Daisy Cake

58

This easy-to-make cake doesn't taste as if it is so simple and quick to prepare.

For enough for a slice for 8 people you will need:

2 eggs

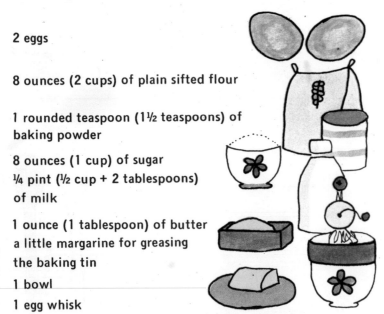

8 ounces (2 cups) of plain sifted flour

1 rounded teaspoon (1½ teaspoons) of baking powder

8 ounces (1 cup) of sugar

¼ pint (½ cup + 2 tablespoons) of milk

1 ounce (1 tablespoon) of butter

a little margarine for greasing the baking tin

1 bowl

1 egg whisk

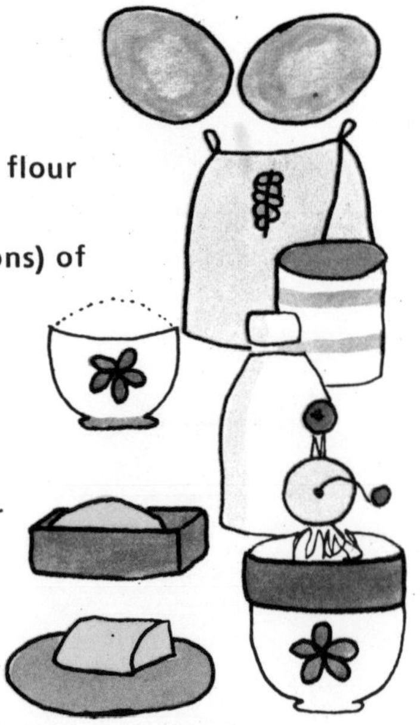

1 saucepan

1 9 inch square deep baking tin (cake pan)

For icing (frosting):

3 ounces (6 tablespoons) of butter

6 ounces (1 cup) of soft brown sugar

2 ounces (½ cup) of chopped walnuts

4 ounces (¾ cup) of grated coconut

1 teaspoon of vanilla essence

1 frying pan (skillet)

1 wooden spoon

ON OVEN
Set the oven at 350°F. Gas Mark 4. Beat the eggs until light and fluffy. Hard work! Add the flour, baking powder and sugar to the eggs and mix well.
It looks a bit odd and lumpy!
Bring the milk and butter to the boil and then add it to the mixt of eggs and flour. Mix well.
Grease the baking tin (pan) and pour in the mixture. Place it in the centre of the oven and cook for 30 minutes. Leave it in the tin (pan) while you prepare the icing (frosting).
Melt the butter in the frying pan (skillet) gently. Add the other ingredients and mix while heatin them slowly. Smooth over the cake in the tin (pan) and place it under a medium grill (broiler) fo 2 minutes. Eat it hot with cream or cold if you can wait!
Watch very ca fully — it will easily overcoo
OVEN OFF

Brown Soda Bread

Country folk in Ireland bake their own bread, and this is how it is done.
Remember to cut it in thicker slices than ordinary bread — and don't spare the butter!

For 2 small loaves — one for today and one for tomorrow — you will need:

12 ounces (3 cups) of wholemeal (whole-wheat) flour

6 ounces (1½ cups) of plain white flour

1 level teaspoon of salt

1 teaspoon of brown sugar

1 heaped teaspoon of baking soda

1 ounce (2 tablespoons) of butter

½ pint (1¼ cups) of buttermilk

a little extra flour for the baking tray

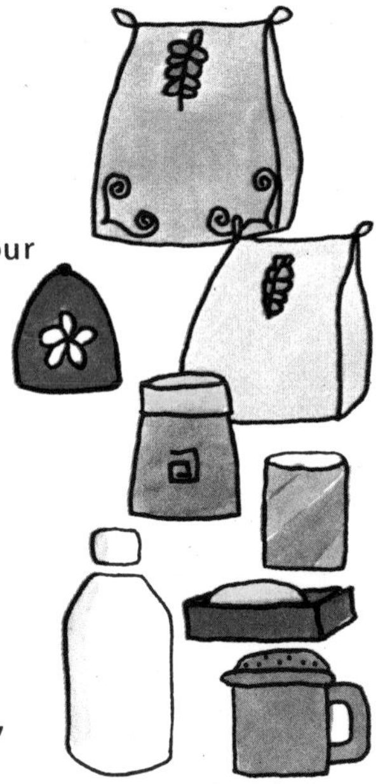

1 large bowl

1 teaspoon

1 fork

1 baking tray (cooky sheet)

1 knife

1 wire rack

ON OVEN
Set the oven at 400°F, Gas Mark 6. Put the flour, salt, sugar and soda into the bowl and mix.
Rub the butter into the flour so that you cannot find it anymore.
Mix the milk into the bowl, using a fork. You may need a little more milk — the dough must be just soft but not gooey.
You may use your hands to get the dough into one round ball.
ke a little flour onto the (sheet). Turn the tray eet) over to get rid of ess flour.
Knead the dough until it is smooth. Make it into two even-sized round shapes. Place them well apart on the baking tray (sheet) and flatten each one with your hand. Make a shallow cross with the knife like this.
Put it into the oven for 30 minutes, middle shelf. Write down the time you put it in. Put the bread on a wire rack to cool, and eat it when it is cold.
OVEN OFF

Pastry – Traditional Method

You can use this pastry dough to make a pie crust for apple pie, jam tarts, meat pies and many other goodies. It is difficult to make at first but you will improve with experience.

For enough dough to make 2 large rounds of pie crust you will need:

12 ounces (3 cups) of flour

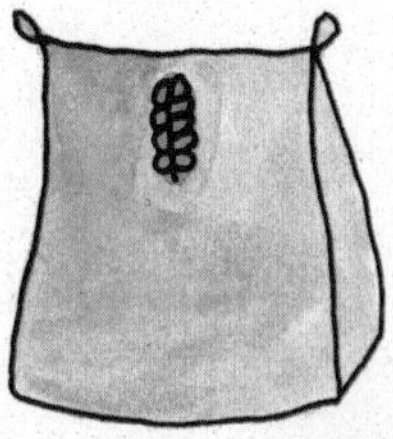

1 level teaspoon of salt

6 ounces (3/4 cup) of cooking fat (shortening)

5 tablespoons (6 1/4 tablespoons) of cold water

2 clean hands!

a little extra flour

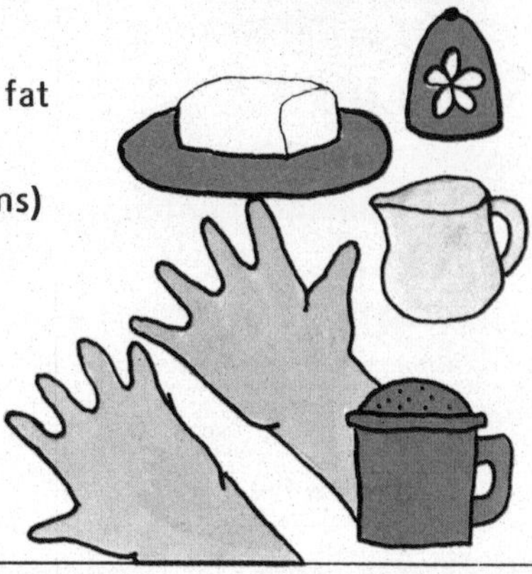

1 sieve

1 large bowl

1 teaspoon

1 knife

1 tablespoon

1 fork

1 rolling pin

Sift the flour and salt into the bowl. Add the fat (shortening).

Using the knife, cut the fat agai the side of the bowl, mixing it with the flour as you cut.

Keep chopping until the fat pieces are the size of a pea.

Now pour the water into the bowl and stir the mixture with a fork. Then use your hands to make it int one round ball. Sprinkle the dough and the rolling pin with flour and roll the pastry out.
Wash your hands.

Pastry - New Fast Method

When you are just beginning to cook you'll enjoy this simple method of making pastry. It tastes very good and you can use it for all the pastry dishes you would like to make.

or enough dough to make 1 large round of pie crust you will need:

ounces (1½ cups) of plain flour

4 tablespoons (5 tablespoons) of oil

2 tablespoons (2½ tablespoons) of water

a pinch of salt

a little extra flour

1 mixing bowl

1 wooden spoon

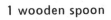

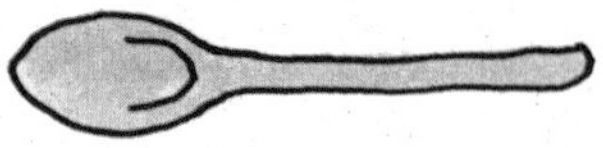

1 rolling pin

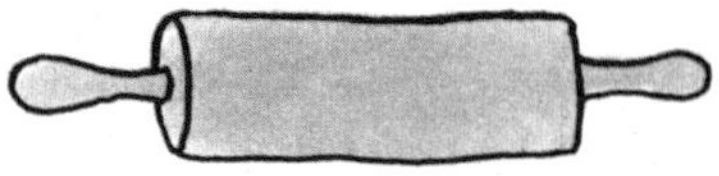

Mix well with the wooden spoon.
Use your hands to put the dough onto a table, sprinkled with flour. Sprinkle flour onto the rolling pin and roll the pastry out.
Use more flour on the table if the pastry begins to stick. Now it is ready to use.

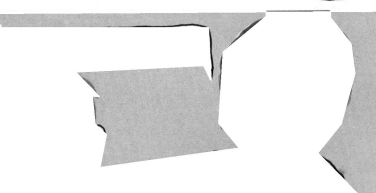

Lemon Meringue Pie

This pie is delicious — everyone I know loves it.

For a pie for 6 people you will need:

a little margarine for greasing the dish

the pastry on page 60 or 61

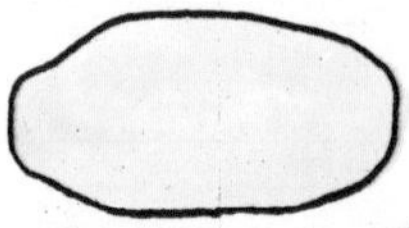

3 lemons, juice and rind

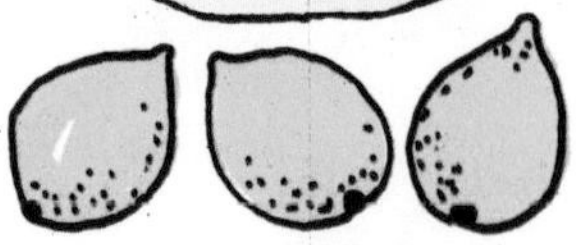

½ pint (1¼ cups) of water

2 ounces (¼ cup) of granulated sugar

2 ounces (½ cup) of cornflour (cornstarch)

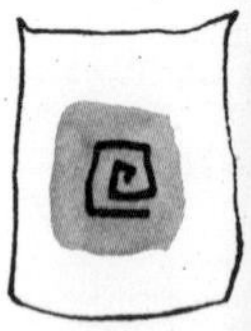

2 eggs

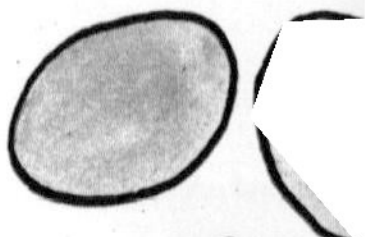

4 ounces (½ cup) of castor sugar (superfine)

a little extra castor sugar

ON OVEN
Set the oven at 425° F, Gas Mark 7. Grease the pie dish with margarine. Cut the pastry to fit the pie dish and prick the pastry with a fork. Bake for 25 minutes. Leave to cool. Turn the oven down to 275° F, Gas Mark 1.
TURN OVEN DOWN

Grate the rind of one of the lemons and then squeeze the three lemons. Boil the water, juice and granulated sugar. Add the lemon rind.

Mix the cornflour (cornstarch) with a little water in a bowl and pour the lemon mixture into the bowl. Mix. Pour back into the saucepan and bring to boiling point, stirring all the time with a wooden spoon. Turn the heat off.

Separate the egg whites and yolks, using the second bowl and the cup.

1 deep pie dish

1 knife

1 fork

1 grater

1 lemon squeezer

1 saucepan

2 small bowls

1 tablespoon

1 wooden spoon

1 cup

1 egg whisk

Add the egg yolks to the mixture in the saucepan and stir well.
No accidents, please!
Pour the lemon mixture into the pastry case. Add the castor sugar (superfine) carefully to the egg whites. Pile the egg whites on top of the lemon mixture, making sure no pastry shows, and make little peaks with the back of a spoon like this.
Everyone you know loves it.
Sprinkle with a little castor sugar (superfine) and bake for 1 hour in the cool (275°F, Gas Mark 1) oven. Serve hot or cold.

Jam Tarts

Jam tarts are favourites with children all over the world.

For 12 tarts you will need:

The pastry on page 60 or 61

extra margarine

a pot of your favourite jam

a little extra flour

1 rolling pin

1 pastry cutter or drinking glass

patty (muffin) tins (for 12 tarts)

1 fork

1 wire rack

1 teaspoon

1 knife

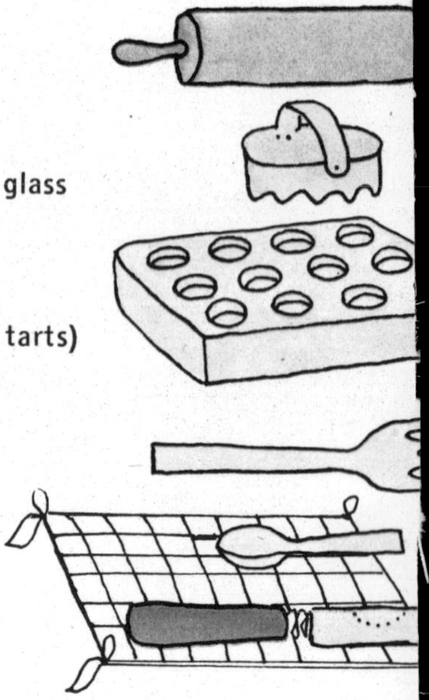

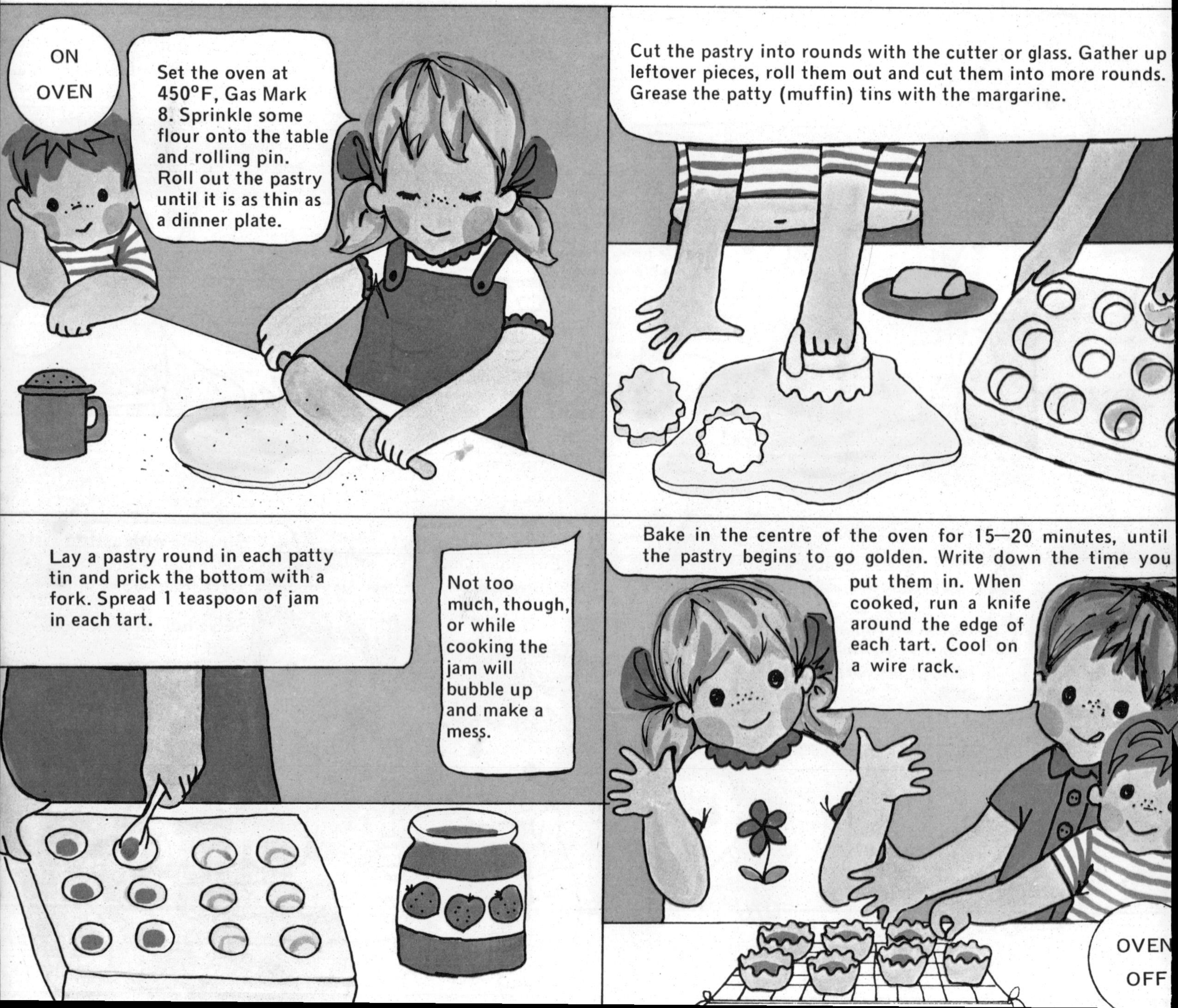

ON OVEN
Set the oven at 450°F, Gas Mark 8. Sprinkle some flour onto the table and rolling pin. Roll out the pastry until it is as thin as a dinner plate.
Cut the pastry into rounds with the cutter or glass. Gather up leftover pieces, roll them out and cut them into more rounds. Grease the patty (muffin) tins with the margarine.
Lay a pastry round in each patty tin and prick the bottom with a fork. Spread 1 teaspoon of jam in each tart.
Not too much, though, or while cooking the jam will bubble up and make a mess.
Bake in the centre of the oven for 15—20 minutes, until the pastry begins to go golden. Write down the time you put them in. When cooked, run a knife around the edge of each tart. Cool on a wire rack.
OVEN OFF